DISCARD

DATE DUE

OCT 0 9 2007	
OCT 1 0 2007	
SEP 1 4 2010	
MAR 2 3 2011	
APR 0 7 2015	

TWENTIETH CENTURY VIEWS

The aim of this series is to present the best in contemporary critical opinion on major authors, providing a twentieth century perspective on their changing status in an era of profound revaluation.

Maynard Mack, *Series Editor*
Yale University

SOPHOCLES

SOPHOCLES

A COLLECTION OF CRITICAL ESSAYS

Edited by
Thomas Woodard

Prentice-Hall, Inc. *Englewood Cliffs, N. J.*

77-8064

Austin Community College
Learning Resources Ce ter

Contents

SOPHOCLES

Introduction

by Thomas Woodard

Sophocles: a familiar name but a hidden face. Successful and esteemed throughout his long career, he is now a forbidding classic. Except occasionally, in the theater, he belongs to the scholar rather than to the public. From time to time a surprised modern reader feels his relevance. But usually he seems remote and elusive; if he leaps out in a flash, he then quickly vanishes back into his reputation. Like Tennyson's Ulysses, he has "become a name." Like his own heroes, he stands on some lonely eminence; his meaning and his strength are enigmatic. A master of irony without an ironic spirit, a humanist while a priest, sober though vehement, a remarkably unpoetic poet: his riddle has proved harder than the Sphinx's.

Along with the riddle, the twentieth century inherited an idealization of Sophocles which can be traced back as far as his sixteenth year in 480 B.C., when the Athenians chose him, because of his exceptional beauty, to lead a dance celebrating the victory of Salamis. During his life he remained famous for charm and grace. After his death, the idealization shifted from physical and social perfection to moral sublimity, and produced an austere, pious, serene Sophocles, oblivious to the harsh particulars of his surroundings. After some twenty-three hundred years, however, the violent discrepancy between this paragon and his dramatic creations was finally noticed—between the ethereal Sophocles and the polluted Oedipus or the pariah Philoctetes. It now seems evident that neoclassicism (whether Alexandrian, Augustan, Renaissance, or Romantic) had formed a classical Sophocles in its own image, shunning the stark plays.

Since World War I the plays have in fact held more fascination

1

than the playwright. Earlier opinions about his character, beliefs, and public service have not so much altered as wilted. The chronology at the back of this volume shows few dates without question marks. Elsewhere our ignorance is even more marked. We have only seven of the original 123 works, and apparently nothing written before the age of fifty. We know that Sophocles served Athens in various capacities and was a friend to Pericles, and that he took part in local cults worshiping heroes. But we do not know in any historically objective way just what his political, ethical, religious, or philosophical attitudes were; some call him conservative, some liberal. And piled on the Pelion of our ignorance is an Ossa of doubt: would more knowledge about Sophocles the Athenian elucidate the plays anyway?

So the twentieth-century Sophocles is, practically speaking, the seven extant plays; and they call for appreciative interpretation. All the authors represented in this volume answer this call, just as Aristotle did in the century after the death of high tragedy in Athens. But Aristotle, on the present view, was satisfied with summary insights into the components, organization, and moral of the plays. Nietzsche, Heidegger, Whitman, and Knox each demand not only a subtler grasp of the inner life of tragedy but also a more potent kind of meaning. Only meaning below the aesthetic and intellectual levels, in the depths of religious or spiritual truth, could be a grail for recent interpretation. But, at the same time, a need almost as strong has been felt to identify this grail with a Grecian urn: a need to see how meaning lives in an artifact capable of sustaining it.

Sophocles began to meet this double demand, for meaning and for art, shortly after World War I, when he was rediscovered on the stage. Max Reinhardt's elaborate productions in Germany (and elsewhere) and Jean Cocteau's trimmed translations in Paris were both important in this revival. By 1930, after composing a rather perverse *Oedipe Roi,* with *voyeur* hero and incestuous children, André Gide could remark to Cocteau, "there is a veritable oedipémie." Cocteau's reply, three years later, was his most brilliant play, *La Machine Infernale,* based on the same legend. Since then, Anouilh's realistic *Antigone* has succeeded in using Greek myth powerfully while reflecting self-consciously on its use; Bertholt

Brecht's modernized productions of *Antigone* and *Oedipus Rex* were perhaps as influential theatrically as his own works; Jean-Paul Sartre's *Les Mouches* (*The Flies*) drew on Sophocles' *Electra* more than on the Aeschylean version of the Orestes story; Ezra Pound's free translation of *Women of Trachis* retracted his earlier gibes at the "rhetoric" and "buncombe" of tragedy; and T. S. Eliot's final play, *The Elder Statesman,* was modeled on the final play of Sophocles, *Oedipus at Colonus.*

With the frequent staging of William Butler Yeats' translation of *King Oedipus* (and its massive audience in the stunning film directed by Tyrone Guthrie), and with the success of truer, more colloquial translations in the 1940s and '50s, an incentive to the reinterpretation of Sophocles continues to spring from the theater and continues to call us back to the theater for which he wrote.

The Athenian theater in the fifth century B.C. was unlike any Western theater after the Middle Ages. Drama meant religious festival, not entertainment alone, and was a civic occasion, not a commercial enterprise. The rarity as well as the ceremony of the productions heightened the spectators' emotions. Performances were restricted to a certain few days a year—holy days, spent in public rites, whether solemn or frenzied. Each play was performed only once in Athens during the dramatist's lifetime. The Sophoclean *oeuvre* therefore came into existence in a context of religious ritual, communal expectancy, and aesthetic hunger.

Clearly, in this context both art and meaning must differ from what we encounter today. Early in the present century English scholars tried to expose the differences by finding primitive origins for tragedy in prehistoric ritual and myth. The Cambridge anthropologists, Fraser, Harrison, Cornford, and others, connected tragic motifs and plots with seasonal cycles and the worship of deities of crop and weather. On this theory, the god of tragedy, Dionysos, whose priest sat in a large stone armchair front-row-center at every performance, played an active though invisible role in the dramas, since he himself represents the divine energy of waxing and waning life.

Neither the meaning nor the form of Sophoclean drama, however, can be adequately appreciated solely in terms of its origins, as various critics have shown; the Cambridge theory, even in its adapta-

tion by Francis Fergusson in *The Idea of a Theater,* would cut
away the complexity of high tragedy and discount its transformation of the old patterns into new, sophisticated works. Nevertheless,
the ritual contents of Sophocles deserve all the attention given them,
even if they are not identical with those of the centuries before him.
For we sense that his imagination renewed contact with the roots
of ritual in nature and worship.

Ritual patterns and the ritual level of action, therefore, remain
a clue to Sophocles. And there is another clue, equally liable to mis-
lead but at least equally important: symbolism. Sophocles integrates
what are for us usually separate spheres of life with symbols: for instance, individuality and universality. In Freudian theory, symbols
translate from the unconscious to the conscious; and interpretation,
whether of dreams or literature, merely retranslates: we do not have
both spheres at once. Largely because of the influence of Freud,
popular opinion expects a symbol to mean something else, something unexpected which we must puzzle out. The Sophoclean symbol, however, means just what it is. It is a character, an event, a
gesture, a word, or a myth, inherently multiple in its implications.
Each play orders the multiplicity; each symbol is conceptually and
imaginatively precise.

Interpretation can claim now that *every* character, event, and
image in Sophoclean drama is symbolic. Every moment in his theater
functions complexly; and each tragedy as a whole forms a larger
symbol.

This suggestion does little more than name a mystery. Still, it is
worth suggesting that Sophoclean drama can be ritual drama (not
just drama in the midst of rituals) because it is symbolic drama. In
chant and dance Greek rituals embodied a felt connection with
invisible forces—forces almost indistinguishably divine, demonic,
instinctual, communal, and physical—that produce the major experiences and patterns of life. To bring these forces onto the stage required more than denotation, pointing or naming: it required a
sensuous, symbolic medium to hold them before our eyes, and to
override the distinction between self and world or between psychology and metaphysics.

In fact, as scholars like F. M. Cornford, Werner Jaeger, Eric
Havelock, J. H. Finley, Jr., and Bruno Snell have stressed, Greek

tragedy thrived before the Greeks explored such distinctions, and before they separated the conceptual from the concrete (as Plato was to do). The language of the fifth century was inevitably symbolic and metaphorical. But, except in choral odes, Sophocles' distinctive style avoids surface metaphors, visual imagery, and similes, employing instead words with several levels of reference hidden below their primary sense in the context. Practically every word in his plays, while springing naturally and directly from dramatic circumstance and characterization, helps develop a number of themes at once. The characters, in other words, say more than they intend or realize; their speech exists in a symbolic world larger than their personalities, the world peculiar to their play.

The world of Greek tragedy was indeed extraordinary, as the productions and their ceremonial settings show. The actors wore special costumes. Why the famous masks? Not for mechanical effects, but to assert that the figures on stage were not ordinary people, to cancel out the face of a man in order to create a personage larger than life, a hero. In the same way and for the same general reason, every play exhibited stylization of gesture, ballet movements, meter, and the alternation of dialogue and lyric.

Modern realistic drama, which still dominates American and British movies, clings to particularity, presses the actor to become sheer personality, and brings out intimately every facial flicker. The Greek masks reject intimacy and present us with a character who is first and foremost a paradigm, an example; who has traits uniquely his own, but to a precisely limited degree. His universality comes naturally to him; he is both organic and impersonal, human and strangely inhuman. We can speak of him only in paradoxes.

Every technique and "convention" of Sophoclean tragedy enforces what is for us its most impressive and most alien quality: architectural unity. The masks and ornate costumes shape large, static figures. The succinctness of each play (which takes little over an hour) allows us to see it as a whole; so too, the memory of an audience trained on oral poetry must have been able to catch this whole simultaneously in a way impossible for us, even with our texts. Furthermore, limitations on the number of actors and on the number of characters taking part in each scene check dispersion and contribute to intelligible form.

Yet this stylized form, seeming almost outside time, embraces the life of the fifth century. The statuesque aspect of Sophocles, insisted upon by Spengler, is no more important than his organic rhythm and sure grasp of action. The dynamic movement of his plots and the vivacity of his characters are evident to a reader or viewer; Sophocles probably owes the larger part of his fame and influence to them. What I wish to stress here, however, is the fusion of static and dynamic in Sophoclean tragedy. There is relevance, it seems to me, in the image of the living temple of Baudelaire's "Correspondances" or the walking statue of Jean Cocteau's poems about Greece. These images imply a wholeness-become-paradox. But Sophocles cultivated wholeness as a birthright. The aesthetic ideals of Phidias and of the Parthenon, already ancient ritual forms, mythological archetypes, and contemporary issues, merged with his inner debates and strongest feelings. The resulting plays bring together the organic and the architectural.

Just as the art of Sophoclean drama reconciles opposing aesthetic tendencies, the most important single clue to its meaning may prove to be an appreciation of how it dramatizes antithetical or contrasting principles, forces, and values. The ancient Greek rituals themselves are said to have done the same. In an *agon* or wrestling match, summer was pitted against winter or an old ruler against a young challenger. The alternation of dialogue and choral ode may suggest, as it did to Nietzsche, a conflict between two gods, Apollo and Dionysos. Within dialogue as well all Greek tragedy springs from pairs: a single actor addressing a chorus, or two actors debating together. Scenes between Antigone and Ismene, Antigone and Creon, Oedipus and Creon, Oedipus and Teiresias, and so on, show such pairings. Even in the scenes with three actors speaking (it was Sophocles who introduced the third actor), pairing still controls, only with a more complicated set of contrasts: for instance, Athena and Odysseus together watch the humiliated Ajax, but Odysseus' sympathy points up the goddess' inhumanity.

Sophoclean heroes define themselves by contrast. They live in an *agon*, they are opposing inimical forces, tested and called to the height of their strength in this struggle. Antigone, Electra, and Philoctetes exist as complements to Creon, Orestes, and Neoptolemos. Heracles and Deianira complement each other in their fatal marriage. Oedipus finds his antagonists in an array of figures, and each brings into the light a new facet of his heroic temper.

This suggests that we cannot fully understand a Sophoclean hero *in himself*. In themselves the heroes usually seem perverse, neurotic, or fanatical. But, just as we see them as symbols of a whole mentality, a world view, a moral code, so in their struggles we see the necessity for their behavior and temperament. They live among agents or powers that would corrupt, break, or ignore their wills. They *must* act as they do; their excesses are justified and virtuous. The heroes live only within their plays; and Sophoclean drama cannot be reduced to their drama alone, as though they were not placed in a larger world—to which, moreover, they are related dialectically.

Recent interpreters have realized that concealed debates, dialectical themes, and symbolic antitheses inform each Sophoclean tragedy. Tradition pays homage to "Sophoclean irony" (a rival of "Socratic irony"), which implies a twofold dramatic situation, known to be twofold by the audience in spite of the fatal delusion of a character like Oedipus that it is simple. We see duality as well in scenic symmetry, as in the two appearances of the guard in *Antigone* or in the two meetings of the sisters in *Electra*. We see it in the "dyptich" structure of *Ajax* and *The Women of Trachis*. And we begin to glimpse a Sophoclean vision of universal struggle between life and death, matter and mind, action and suffering.

Polemos panton pater: conflict fathers everything. Along with his older contemporaries, Heraclitus, Empedocles, Parmenides, and Anaxagoras, Sophocles saw a clash of opposites giving an intelligible while dynamic pattern to all change and natural process. His special achievement seems to be the dramatization of this cosmos as it informs human experience, as it affects and centers around man the whole being, not man the wise mind of the philosophers. For these talk of the war of equal opposites but affirm in the last analysis only *logos*—discourse, reason—or *nous*—intelligence, mind; they affirm in the last analysis only their own talk and thought. Sophocles, however, embraces action as fervently as language; his plays tangibly unite the two.

Sophocles was a dramatist (rather than philosopher or lyric poet) because he found dialectical principles and forces *alive,* and alive only *in* action and passion, *in* human dilemmas, *in* nature, community, and history. We realize now that the Greek terms for these principles play a central role in each of the tragedies: *polis,* the city, the society, *and* the state; *nomos,* law *and* custom; *physis,* nature, the organic, *and* an individual's identity; *theos,* divinity or a god; *logos,* talk, thought, reputation, reason; *kakos,* low-born, base, evil, evils, ills; *ergon,* act, fact, work; *dike,* justice, human or divine, a penalty or a goddess, redress and balance.

These terms were part of the vast inheritance of suggestive language that Sophocles entered into at birth. But he made each function as a metaphor; he drew on multiple meanings and played one off against another. Each tragedy is ordered around different terms and each defines its own terms. We are only beginning to feel their distinctively Sophoclean sense. Many of the essays in this volume make precisely that beginning. It is for them to interpret the plays singly. But a few general remarks about the relationship between Sophocles' dialectical universe and his largest symbols, the heroes, may help prepare for the more detailed analyses.

The Sophoclean heroes live on the edge of humanity. They constantly assert their individuality, nobility, freedom, and strength. Several live apart from society quite literally: Ajax in his solitary tent by the sea, Philoctetes marooned on a desert island, Oedipus the beggar without a country. All act completely on their own, out of passionate motives that ultimately defy rational comprehension; all willingly incur the charges of insanity, blindness, and folly. Their irreducible, unconquerable moral resolve usually hides its roots, so that they resemble their modern, existentialist progeny, such as Anouilh's *entêtée* Antigone, or Camus' absolutistic Caligula. Ajax—isolated, spurned, shamed—prefers death to a compromised life, just as Antigone and Electra become cold and bitter rather than prostitute themselves before injustice. The resistance of all the heroes to evil, their living death, and their active passion, which may seem to spring from some private conscience, have their origin, however, in cosmic forces, cosmic truths. Modern adapters and interpreters have often failed to see this ground of the heroic morality, have failed to see how each hero symbolizes something of eternity, divine wrath, divine alienation. Death, especially, is the heroes' dominion—five of them voluntarily die or attempt suicide—because it represents the end of mere mortality and is a godlike alternative to a corrupt life. The heroes seek a timelessness akin to the changeless repetition of ritual; their morals reflect worship and divine presence. And all have direct contact with *logos,* spiritual truth beyond appearances, which manifests itself in their potent, authoritative utterances: curses, oaths, refusals, commands.

Yet these heroes, with their affinity to a divine and unearthly world, are also intensely earthy and impassioned, more deeply rooted in the truths of blood, family, honor, and instinct, than their antagonists. For they all represent *physis,* nature informing their natures; and Sophoclean *physis* is eternal and divine. In their death they are born in spirit, like the *daemons* worshiped in Greek hero cults; so *physis* dies and revives each year like Dionysos. The eternity of *physis* is thus cyclical, and resembles liturgy. Sophoclean *logos,* furthermore, is the apprehension of *physis* by participation in its rhythms; *logos* is the way that *physis* reveals itself to man. *Logos* therefore expresses wholeness in nature; implies the integration of the faculties; implies the union of human and cosmic. The Sophoclean heroes' intuitive awareness of their own *physis,* their realization of their own *logos,* unites them to universal *physis* and *logos* and allows them to withstand all the powers of temptation, public opinion, and human malice.

These heroic figures redefine all moral problems, because they act in a dimension beyond ordinary conscious life. To her fight with Creon, Antigone brings not only anger, daring, and pride, but a felt union with chthonian divinities, an allegiance to the conservative politics of family and clan, and also the power and necessity of *physis* and universal *dike*(Creon matches her with his own anger, stubbornness, and pride,) with his faith in intellect and in the Olympian gods of state religion, with his narrow but sensible democratic optimism, his concern for the *polis,* and his commitment to man-made *nomoi. Dike* naturally wins out in the end. We refuse to mourn the death of Antigone, since it perfects her heroism; but the justice that justifies her inspires us with awe. The rending antitheses of the *Antigone* reach no "synthesis" or "resolution": unless through a fuller participation in the macrocosm which generates them. And witnessing Sophocles' drama is such participation.

The world of Sophocles' tragedies is remote; Sophocles' tragedies are moving, lifelike, and tough-minded, they are complex and capacious in a way our critical language cannot fully grasp. I have tried to suggest this in discussing some Sophoclean themes. Words like "hero," "justice," or "nature" almost inevitably give the modern reader a false impression. Another good example lies closer to hand, in the one term always applied to this drama: tragedy. In the first place, probably none of the seven are "tragedies" in the common Elizabethan (and twentieth century) sense of a study in downfall, which apparently derives from the theory of Aristotle and the practice of Euripides. The "downfall" of the Sophoclean hero can be found only in *Oedipus Rex,* and even there, as Bernard Knox maintains, Oedipus has, by the end, reclaimed much of his original authority and independence. In another way, too, the term "tragedy" is inadequate: each work has multiple qualities of atmosphere and dramatic style. Strictly speaking, the proper name for the *genre* of each is the proper name of the play. *Philoctetes* is a problem play, turning on moral issues explicitly raised in the Prologue; its twists of plot, its villain, and its surprise happy ending resemble modern melodrama; yet it is also a formal heroic pageant, set against the backdrop of a symbolic landscape. *Oedipus at Colonus* is a passion play leading to apotheosis, a psychological study, a political debate, and a local epic. Similarly with the others. None are what our critical vocabulary leads us to expect or enables us to categorize simply.

With the complexity of Sophocles in mind, we may view attempts to interpret him with a more sympathetic eye. His world seems remote even from that of Aristotle's *Poetics* in the next century. Aristotle awards Sophocles a permanent first prize as playwright and draws many of his central concepts from *Oedipus Rex.* But, while singling out this work for praise, the philosopher notes only a few salient features of its plot and dramaturgy. The *Poetics,* of course, aims at more than an analysis of Sophocles; but insofar as it interprets him at all its language is not his but Aristotle's own. The result, as C. H. Whitman forcefully argues, was that a small group of philosophical terms controlled discussion about Sophocles until the end of the nineteenth century. Since Aristotle appeared to find an exclusively ethical message in *Oedipus Rex,* such notions as *hybris* (pride, violence, excess) and *hamartia* (flaw, mistake, sin) served for centuries as explanations for the supposed fall of the hero, and eventually Christianized Sophocles, making him an apostle of humility. Such a Sophocles was lukewarm, and less interesting than his rivals ancient and modern. So, ironically, Aristotle contributed to a decline in Sophocles' literary standing, though the blame should not be laid on the *Poetics* but on the way it was read as Scripture.

At the beginning of the present century, the bulky, scrupulous, line by line commentary of Sir R. C. Jebb effectively re-established the text and the academic importance of Sophocles, but hardly ventured into general interpretation. Since Jebb, and continuing to use Jebb's work, the study of Sophocles has gradually undergone a reformation like that of the study of modern literature. It has shown an increasing concern for interpretation, as distinct from textual or biographical problems, and has changed its ideals and methods of interpretation. Details of this evolution and of its philosophical bases lie beyond my present topic. So also does an analysis of the "philological" or "historical" approaches that ruled classical scholarship, at least in English, until the 1950s. As background for this volume, it suffices to begin by saying that already in the 1930s there were radical attempts to read without traditional presuppositions. In 1933 Karl Reinhardt published his *Sophokles,* with a chapter on each play, and in 1936 Martin Heidegger delivered the lecture on the *Antigone* reprinted in this volume. Heidegger and, to a lesser extent, Reinhardt challenged not only prevailing theories about meaning in the dramas but also prevailing conceptions of meaning itself. As Heidegger's other writings on Greek thought show, he claims historical authenticity for his interpretations. In part, however, he rejects previous definitions of historical authenticity; and, in part, he believes that the original sense of the ancient Greek was lost through fallacious translation into Latin (and, subsequently, the modern languages). The work of Reinhardt and the phenomenological approach developed by Heidegger are still probably the most influential on the continent of Europe.

In 1939 H. D. F. Kitto with great literary finesse offered British scholarship new views on all the Greek tragedies. Kitto discussed classical drama on the assumption that the same aesthetic concepts apply to it as to modern literature. He read each play as a unique artifact; he kept dramatic poetry distinct from chronicle, philosophy, or lyric. Despite the rather cavalier brevity of its analysis of each play, Kitto's *Greek Tragedy* deserved more recognition than it received in the 1940s. But Kitto's influence has steadily increased. And now, though his interpretations are rarely accepted in detail, his critical approach almost seems standard in England and America.

Because Kitto's writings are so well known and so easily obtainable, no sample has been included in this collection. For the same reason, it is natural to treat him as a point of departure in mentioning other recent good work. Kitto justifiably emphasized the "conscious artistry," the rational control, behind the plays during the years when a concern for their unconscious or subliminal sources was emerging in scholarship. The original study of *The Imagery of Sophocles' Antigone* by R. F. Goheen drew on New Critical assumptions about poetry and traced a number of submerged patterns of meaning by examining the play's vocabulary. The results were somewhat inconclusive, but Goheen's approach clearly implied that most previous interpretations had been superficial. C. H. Whitman's *Sophocles* also broke new ground and undermined many received opinions about the impact of the plays in the fifth century; it found a coherent, passionate philosophy of religious humanism in the heroic figures and plots of all seven tragedies.

These two books used very different critical techniques, but both described a playwright whose sensibility and intentions bear little resemblance to Kitto's master craftsman with an intelligible scheme. Goheen was interested in how Sophocles' metaphorical language suggests more than its primary meanings; the plays are essentially verbal works. For Whitman, on the other hand, the plays are more plastic; their action is more important than their language; and they are mainly vehicles for the hero's moral qualities, qualities which elevate him so far above his fellows that he gains a kind of inward divinity. Kitto is more rationalistic than either. Pursuing his method of deducing meaning from form, he at times overemphasizes details, at times reduces meaning to merely general propositions. But he keeps precise dramatic effects more vividly in mind than Goheen or Whitman, and keeps closer to the total logic of each play.

Proof that the approaches and, to some extent, the conclusions of Goheen, Whitman, and Kitto may be reconciled has come in the last ten years with the work of Bernard M. W. Knox. His interpretations seize on both the metaphorical and the logical complexity of Sophocles' language without belaboring the question of where conscious intention ends and creative instinct begins. His practice treats form with the flexibility that Kitto demands on principle. And he elicits meaning that reflects every facet of fifth century history and experience. His latest book, *The Heroic Temper*—essays on the recurrent traits of the Sophoclean hero and on several individual plays—continues the demonstration, in his *Oedipus at Thebes*, that the heroes embody recognizable Athenian moral, political, and cultural ideals, while it points up their idiosyncrasies and individualism.

The major products of recent scholarly interest in Sophocles will probably hold their place as classics of literary criticism: Whitman's broad, stimulating conception of fifth-century "heroic humanism" and heroic religiosity; Kitto's treatment of Sophoclean *dike* and his suggestive pages on individual plays; Knox's cogent analyses of five of the seven extant tragedies and his portrayal of the heroes. These interpreters, and others in this volume, show that erudition can serve imagination and that the most impressive results spring from minds encountering the Greek freshly, as if at the original productions.

Encountering the Greek: then what about those not knowing Greek? Reassurance to the general reader cannot go very far on this question. Sophocles means his language; the Greekless reader reads a translator's language. And the inevitable gap between translation and original (the gap between two different *kinds* of language, as well as between two different civilizations) can widen indefinitely. As T. S. Eliot remarked about a translator of the early part of the century: "Professor Murray has simply interposed between Euripides and ourselves a barrier more impenetrable than the Greek language."

However, the Greekless reader should not feel like the Keats that Yeats imagined "with face and nose pressed to a sweet-shop window." Translations give many of the essentials of dramatic effect and larger meaning; they give an immediate reaction that Greek usually makes impossible. The scholar's interpretations may claim a fidelity to the ancient text that the general reader can scarcely judge. But the quality of the scholar's response matters more than the quantity of his erudition.

Personal encounters with Sophocles, often without rigorous attention to the text, probably lie behind what many philosophers say about him. Instructively enough, philosophers of this century assimilate literature to their own ends even more than Aristotle and Hegel did. Freud appropriates *Oedipus Rex* for his "universally valid" doctrine of sexuality; Spengler uses the same play to demonstrate the corporeality of the Greek spirit. And Simone Weil could write admiringly:

> Sophocles is the Greek poet whose inspiration is most visibly and perhaps most finely Christian. (He is much more Christian than any tragic poet of the last twenty centuries, to my knowledge.) This quality is generally recognized in the tragedy of *Antigone,* which might be an illustration of the saying "It is better to obey God than men." The God present in that tragedy is not imagined in the heavens but under the earth, among the dead. But it amounts to the same thing. What is always at issue is the true God, the God in the other world.[1]

Logical and historical fallacies: yet their very obviousness touches us, by seeming to bring out in the open a mind's first efforts at making alien thought its own. Or is the naïveté disingenuous? Are we not led to reflect on Simone Weil's assumptions about the possibilities of historically valid interpretation? For if Christian revelation is "universally valid," then may not the *Antigone* glimpse it? And, conversely, if the *Antigone* contains a Christian message, may not Christian revelation be universally valid? In this way, the "interpretations" of Weil, Freud, or Spengler lure us onto the philosopher's own ground, and make us consider a work in terms of issues quite possibly foreign to it and certainly foreign to most literary scholarship. But for just this reason, such courageous oversimplifications have at least half a chance of bringing us closer to essentials than we might otherwise come.

Since scholars have no exclusive title to Sophocles, and everyone should confidently take up his text and read, we might expect that

---

[1] *Intuitions Pré-Chrétiennes* (Paris: Editions du Vieux Colombier, 1951), p. 18. Editor's translation.

many twentieth-century authors—besides philosophers and critics—would have done so and then voiced their reactions. But Sophocles' Greek and Sophocles' reputation have kept most modern literary writers from writing about him at all. Although D. H. Lawrence, while composing *Sons and Lovers,* called *Oedipus Rex* "the finest drama of *all* times," and although Jean Cocteau's first volume of verse was *La Danse de Sophocle,* neither commented on the playwright publicly. Nor did T. S. Eliot, James Joyce, André Gide, Thomas Mann, William Butler Yeats, or Samuel Beckett. Only Virginia Woolf wasn't afraid of Sophocles.

Therefore, in this collection Sophocles speaks mainly in dialogue with philosophers and Hellenists. And these essays are primarily attempts to elicit meaning from art. It has doubtless seemed especially urgent in recent decades to reclaim, through reinterpretation, the masterpieces of our heritage. Sophocles' revival in the theater (in translation and adaptation), and our reformed sense of his vision, promise that he will continue to give food for thought and spirit out of the concealed roots of his creativity. This anthology should assist us to receive what he offers. But it will also suggest, I believe, that the seven plays hold truth for which Sophocles found words as we cannot.

Sophoclean Tragedy

by Friedrich Nietzsche

Everything which comes to the surface in dialogue (the Apollonian half of Greek tragedy) looks simple, transparent, beautiful. Thus dialogue reproduces the Hellene who reveals his nature in the dance. In the dance because there the greatest energy is potential, only betrayed by smoothness and variety of movement. The language of Sophoclean heroes surprises us with its Apollonian directness and clarity, so much that we immediately suppose ourselves looking to the very ground of their being—and with some astonishment that the path could be so short. But if we glance away from whatever, becoming visible, comes to the surface as heroic character (but with no more physical depth than an image of light projected on a dark ground, i.e., an *apparition* through and through), we penetrate into the source of this brilliant projection, the myth, and suddenly experience the opposite of a well known optical effect. When we make a determined effort to hold the sun in our eyes we turn away blinded but at once darkly colored spots dance before us to heal our eyes. Reverse this: those apparitions of light, the Sophoclean heroes, in short the Apollonian expressing itself through masks, are necessary products of looking into the arcana and terrors of Nature, shining spots come to heal eyes seared by that harrowing dark. And it is only thus that we dare believe that we have rightly understood the meaningful concept of "Greek serenity"—yet at every turn now we meet its misinterpretation as a state of unthreatened good feeling.

The most pathetic figure of the Greek theater, the unfortunate Oedipus, Sophocles takes to be a noble man called to error and

"Sophoclean Tragedy" by Friedrich Nietzsche. From *The Birth of Tragedy.* Translated for this volume by Michael Lebeck.

alienation in spite of his wisdom, yet called too, in the end, through monstrous suffering, to radiate a magic power rich in a blessing which works even after he passes on. "The noble man does not sin" is what the poet means. Though every natural law, the whole civilized world, fall to the ground through his actions, these very actions attract a higher, magical circle of influences which grounds a new world upon the rubble of the old. This is what the poet— inasmuch as he is a religious thinker—means. As a poet he begins by presenting a marvelously complicated legal tangle which his hero, as judge, decides slowly, piece by piece—to his own undoing! The truly Hellenic joy in the dialectics of decision is so great that it deploys a superior force of serenity which occupies the whole work, everywhere blunting the points of the horrifying assumptions of this case. In the *Oedipus at Colonus* we meet this same serenity— but transfigured to endless heights: over against that old man upon whom the cup of alienation has overflowed, who is given as a trophy to all that overtakes him, sufferer absolute, stands this inhuman serenity which descends from divine spheres and suggests to us that it is in absolute passivity that the hero achieves greatest activity, reaching far beyond the end of his life, while the intentional hustling of his earlier years led him nowhere but to this. Hence the problems chaotically knotted together into the tale of Oedipus, to mortal eye insoluble, are slowly sorted out—and the profoundest human joy overwhelms us in the dialectical reversal due to the gods. Even if this interpretation does the poet justice, one is still justified in asking if thereby the substance of the myth has been exhausted: and here we find demonstrated that the whole conception of the poet is nothing other than that "image of light," with which, after our look into the Abyss, healing Nature confronts us. Oedipus who murders his father and marries his mother. Oedipus who solves the riddle of the Sphinx! What does this mysterious trinity of fateful deeds tell us? An ancient legend, occurring in purest form among the Persians, relates that a wise magician is born only as a result of incest—which, looking back to Oedipus, riddle-solver, wooer of his mother, we cannot hesitate to explicate as follows: wherever the bonds between Present and Future, the rigid law of individuation, and the enchantment which Nature casts over us are broken by prophetic or magical powers, the cause must be in some monstrous crime (as incest here) which has already been committed against Nature—for would Nature have bestowed upon man the trophy of her Mysteries if not compelled to do so by his having gone victoriously against her grain, i.e., by *unnatural* means? This realization I find impressed upon the horrifying trinity of the Oedipal destiny: the very man who solves Nature's riddle (Nature, the Sphinx who combines two natures) must also as father's murderer and mother's husband transgress the most holy laws of Nature. Indeed this myth appears to insinuate that wisdom, and Dionysian wisdom in particular, is an unnatural abomination, that the man who by means of his learning trips Nature into the annihilating Abyss must also experience Nature's dissolution in himself. "The point of wisdom turns of itself against the wise, Wisdom is a crime against Nature"—such terrifying sentences reach us from this myth. The Hellenic poet however touches the awesome Memnon of mythology like a ray of sunlight and suddenly the monument begins to ring—with a Sophoclean music! To the glory of passivity I now oppose the glory of activity. It illuminates Prometheus in Aeschylus. What Aeschylus as thinker would have told us but what as a poet he only leaves us to guess at from his metaphorical creation, this the youthful Goethe could make plain in his "Prometheus" with these audacious words:

> I sit here moulding mankind
> After my image,
> A race like unto me
> In suffering, in sorrow,
> In enjoyment and rejoicing
> And with no respect, Zeus, for *you*—
> Like myself!

Concentrating the essence of his humanity man becomes Titanic: thus he wins his culture for himself and compels the gods to ally themselves with him, since it is a wisdom all his own which has delivered the certainty of their existence, and of their limitations, into his hand. But the most marvelous thing about the earlier *Prometheus* (according to its shaping idea Impiety's truest hymn) is the powerful attraction which justice has for Aeschylus: the immeasurable suffering of the bold "Individual" to the one side, to the other the Divine in difficulties, yes, the gods suspicious of their final passing—the compelling authority of two worlds of suffering leads to conciliation, to metaphysical identity. All this forcibly calls to mind the keystone, the chief thesis of Aeschylean cosmology which sees above gods and man Moira upon a throne, Eternal Justice. Because of the astonishing boldness with which Aeschylus places the Olympian world upon the balance of Justice, we must keep in mind how irreversibly fixed was the substratum of metaphysical thinking the Greek received in his Mysteries, and that all his impulsive skepticisms could be discharged upon the Olympians. Among the Greeks the artist in particular felt in looking back to these divinities, obscurely, the reciprocal working of dependence. And in the very person of Aeschylus' Prometheus this feeling becomes symbol. The Titan artist had found within himself the obstinate faith in his ability to create mankind and at least to bring the Olympians to nothing—and this by means of a higher wisdom, admittedly compelling payment of eternal suffering. This lordly "ability" of the great genius, cheap even at the price of eternal suffering, this acid pride of the *artist*—that is what the Aeschylean poem is all about, while Sophocles with his Oedipus strikes up the prelude to a victory hymn for the *saint*.

Tragedy: Classical *vs.* Western

by Oswald Spengler

It follows from the meaning that we have attached to the
Culture as a prime phenomenon and to destiny as the organic logic
of existence, that each Culture must necessarily possess its own
destiny-idea. Indeed, this conclusion is implicit from the first in the
feeling that every great Culture is nothing but the actualizing and
form of a single, singularly-constituted (einzigartig) soul. And what
cannot be felt by one sort of men exactly as it is felt by another
(since the life of each is the expression of the idea *proper* to himself) and still less transcribed, what is named by us "conjuncture,"
"accident," "Providence," or "Fate," by Classical man "Nemesis,"
"Ananke," "Tyche," or "Fatum," by the Arab "Kismet," by everyone
in some way of his own, is just that of which each unique and un-
reproduceable soul-constitution, quite clear to those who share in it,
is a rendering.

The Classical form of the Destiny-idea I shall venture to call
Euclidean. Thus it is the sense-actual person of Oedipus, his "em-
pirical ego," nay, his σῶμα that is hunted and thrown by Destiny.
Oedipus complains that Creon has misused his "body" and that the
oracle applied to his "body." Aeschylus, again, speaks of Agamemnon
as the "royal body, leader of fleets." It is this same word σῶμα that
the mathematicians employ more than once for the "bodies" with
which they deal. But the destiny of King Lear is of the "analytical"
type—to use here also the term suggested by the corresponding
number-world—and consists in dark inner relationships. The idea

of fatherhood emerges; spiritual threads weave themselves into
the action, incorporeal and transcendental, and are weirdly illuminated by the counterpoint of the secondary tragedy of Gloucester's
house. Lear is at the last a mere name, the axis of something un-
bounded. *This* conception of destiny is the "infinitesimal" conception. It stretches out into infinite time and infinite space. It
touches the bodily Euclidean existence not at all, but affects only
the Soul. Consider the mad King between the fool and the outcast
in the storm on the heath, and then look at the Laocoön group;
the first is the Faustian, the other the Apollinian way of suffering.
Sophocles, too, wrote a Laocoön drama; and we may be certain
that there was nothing of *pure soul-agony* in it. Antigone goes below
ground in the body, because she has buried her brother's body.
Think of Ajax and Philoctetes, and then of the Prince of Homburg
and Goethe's Tasso—is not the difference between magnitude and
relation traceable right into the depths of artistic creation?

This brings us to another connection of high symbolic significance.
The drama of the West is ordinarily designated *Character-Drama.*
That of the Greeks, on the other hand, is best described as *Situation-
Drama,* and in the antithesis we can perceive what it is that Western,
and what it is that Classical, man, respectively, feel as the basic
life-form that is imperiled by the onsets of tragedy and fate. If in
lieu of "direction" we say "irreversibility," if we let ourselves sink
into the terrible meaning of those words "too late" wherewith we
resign a fleeting bit of the present to the *eternal* past, we find the
deep foundation of every tragic crisis. It is Time that is the tragic,
and it is by the meaning that it intuitively attaches to Time
that one Culture is differentiated from another; and consequently
"tragedy" of the grand order has only developed in the Culture
which has most passionately affirmed, and in that which has most
passionately denied, Time. The sentiment of the ahistoric soul gives
us a Classical tragedy of the moment, and that of the ultrahistorical
soul puts before us Western tragedy that deals with the *development
of a whole life.* Our tragedy arises from the feeling of an *inexorable
Logic* of becoming, while the Greek feels the *illogical, blind Casual
of the moment*—the life of Lear matures inwardly toward a catastrophe, and that of Oedipus stumbles without warning upon a situation. And now one may perceive how it is that synchronously with

Western drama there rose and fell a mighty portrait-art (culminating in Rembrandt), a kind of historical and biographical art which (*because* it was so) was sternly discountenanced in Classical Greece at the apogee of Attic drama. Consider the veto on likeness-statuary in votive offerings and note how—from Demetrius of Alopeke (about 400)—a timid art of "ideal" portraiture began to venture forth when, and only when, grand tragedy had been thrown into the background by the light society-pieces of the "Middle Comedy." Fundamentally all Greek statues were standard masks, like the actors in the theatre of Dionysos; all bring to expression, in significantly strict form, *somatic* attitudes and positions. Physiognomically they are *dumb,* corporeal and *of necessity* nude—character-heads of definite individuals came only with the Hellenistic age. Once more we are reminded of the contrast between the Greek number-world, with its computations of tangible results, and the other, our own, in which the relations between groups of functions or equations or, generally, formula-elements of the same order are investigated morphologically, and the character of these relations fixed *as such* in express laws.

Thought and Structure
in Sophoclean Tragedy

by Robert D. Murray, Jr.

Because we are men of the twentieth century and not of the fifth century B.C., there are obviously many obstacles between us and a proper confrontation of Greek tragedy. Not the least of these roadblocks is the fact that as men of the twentieth century we have been exposed often to a critical doctrine that does not meet the facts of the case. This doctrine, paralleled and perhaps even stimulated by movements in music, the fine arts, and philosophy, informs us that we are stumbling into an intellectual bog if we try to look for moral or meaning in a literary work. The projection of a moral view is not centrally a function of the work of art; after all, if one wishes to convey meaning and morality verbally, this end can be accomplished most precisely and unambiguously through the precision of prose discourse. Poetry, perhaps since Dante, has seldom been regarded as the best vehicle for earnest and profound communication of significant ethical and religious views.

A Greek of the fifth century would, of course, have felt very differently about the matter. He would not have objected at all to the presence of morality, didacticism, even "messages" in poetry, and especially the drama. Indeed, he felt that moral instruction was a vital and valuable function of tragic drama, in particular, and that the voice of the poet was the voice of morality and wisdom as well as of beauty. Indeed, it was an habitual tendency of the Greek mind to identify beauty and good, or rather to accept this identification without any question (in any dictionary of ancient Greek, the adjective *kalos* will be translated as "beautiful, good, genuine, virtuous, noble, honorable"; its opposite, *kakos,* as "ugly,

cowardly, base, bad, evil"). This attitude is clearly reflected in the
fifth-century view toward any form of art; that which is beautiful
must be morally good, and that which is evil must of necessity also
be ugly. Aesthetic pleasure and moral instruction are truly one and
inseparable, a unity soon to be recognized by Aristotle in his recurrent emphasis on the moral character of the kind of agents fitted
for tragic drama, and in the more ethical aspects of his *catharsis*.
To sum up, the Greeks of the fifth century and well into the fourth
were convinced that poetry, especially tragedy, is essentially moral;
that there is meaning in the drama, and that meaning is closely
related to the aesthetic impact of the whole. Thus, to the contemporaries of Sophocles, a poet was expected to express a view of
life, even a "message." Had he not done so, he would have failed
his audiences. Had they thought he had not done so, he would not
have won prizes in the Theater of Dionysos. But did Sophocles
truly play the game within the rules established by his cultural
tradition? Did he instruct as well as delight, adorn charm with
wisdom? Do the tragedies embody an earnest view of life, or are
they only exciting and superbly devised re-enactments of impossible
situations, designed to absorb our emotions for a couple of hours,
and send us out the aisles in some kind of limp and exhausted
state of purification?

Agreement on this issue, in our time, appears to be out of reach;
the spectrum of Sophoclean criticism has broadened noticeably
in recent years. Let C. M. Bowra speak for the moralists:[1]

> The central idea of a Sophoclean tragedy is that through suffering
> a man learns to be modest before the gods. . . . When [the char-
> acters] are finally forced to see the truth, we know that the gods have
> prevailed and that men must accept their own insignificance.

In short, for Bowra, the essence of each play of Sophocles is a
message urging humility and piety. The poet wants to teach us
something important, and he does it effectively.

For the formalists, A. J. A. Waldock answers the moralists with
appealing indignation, in his discussion of the *Oedipus Tyrannus*:[2]

---

[1] C. M. Bowra, *Sophoclean Tragedy* (London: Oxford Univ. Press, 1944), pp.
365-66.
[2] A. J. A. Waldock, *Sophocles the Dramatist* (London: Cambridge Univ. Press,
1951), pp. 167-68.

We know little of Sophocles' religion. When we sum up what we know of his beliefs we find them meagre in number and depressingly commonplace in quality. . . . He believed that there are ups and downs in fortune, and that men are never secure. . . . There is religion in the *Oedipus Tyrannus,* but it is not all crucial in the drama. . . . *There is no meaning in the Oedipus Tyrannus* [italics mine]. There is merely the terror of coincidence, and then, at the end of it all, our impression of man's power to suffer, and of his greatness because of this power.

Now Waldock's reaction is surely a needed response to the ultra-moralistic notion that Sophocles was driven by an urge to warn his contemporaries that they should not be rash or proud lest a vengeful heaven strike them down, and eager to communicate this unsuual advice, set it in open code in the story of Oedipus. But as so often, reaction becomes overreaction; it is hard to believe, with the extreme formalist, that the playwright was little interested in attitudes and values, but only in dramatic or even theatrical display; that any meaning is a *parergon,* coincidental to brilliance of structure, and without organic relationship to form. What sensitive audience could view the *Oedipus Tyrannus* and leave the theater not wondering why this man had to suffer what he suffered, and why the gods played the role they unquestionably played? (No degree of post-Verrallian ingenuity can dismiss the entrance of the Corinthian messenger, an instant after Jocasta's prayer to Apollo, as sheer coincidence.) In fact, to accept the formalist attitude without qualification is to accuse Sophocles of a serious artistic blunder—he has *compelled* his audience to absorb itself in ethical and spiritual considerations that have little or nothing to do with his genuine dramatic aims! He has diverted the attention of the viewer from dramatic form and power to unintended commonplaces.

To return to Waldock. He regards the *Tyrannus,* produced perhaps in 428, as a superb exercise in structure, a moving masterpiece of theater, an intricate piece of machinery designed to startle, dazzle, and shock (perhaps a little like the self-destructive machines that have recently been exhibited in our contemporary museums). But as having no serious meaning.

Some twenty-two years later, Sophocles died, just having written his last play, *Oedipus at Colonus.* Was this another experiment in structural virtuosity, without any hard center of meaning? To a degree, says Waldock; now the old Sophocles, attracted by the theme of the death of Oedipus (comparably old, in poetic terms) was faced with the necessity of stretching out, with dramatic or near-melo-dramatic tensions, a story that did not really contain enough stuff for a play. Within certain limits, the theme seems to dictate struc-ture, but exciting inventions are needed to keep the plot going. Thus the involvements (Creon, Polyneices) in the central portion of the play, where the main theme, the apotheosis of Oedipus, seems to stutter and fairly grinds to a halt. The scholar's argument seems reasonable. If it is right, we must conclude that much of the *Oedipus at Colonus* is compelling theater, but not highly serious, organically unified drama.

An amusing myth has invaded and established itself in certain areas of the academic world: that Sophocles composed a Theban *trilogy; Oedipus Tyrannus, Oedipus at Colonus,* and *Antigone.* This despite the odd fact that the production of the third preceded the first by about thirteen years, that the second followed the first by about twenty-two, and that the problems of the Antigone are in many ways so alien to those of the later plays. I suspect that the intrusion of the myth has persuaded many teachers besides myself to raise a storm warning for our students: "beware of interpreting any one of the Theban plays in terms of another." This signal of danger is surely soundly displayed. But in the case of the two Oedipus plays, the warning may lead to excessive caution. While a much older Sophocles wrote the *Oedipus at Colonus,* it was surely a Sophocles who recalled vividly the dramatic problems he had struggled with in the *Oedipus Tyrannus,* and who might well ex-pect the mature element of his audience to remember the form and impact of the earlier play.

A comparison of the structure of the two later Theban plays strongly suggests that this supposition is accurate. To a startling degree, the *Oedipus at Colonus* seems to mirror the formal design of the *Oedipus Tyrannus,* and to reverse it in mirror fashion.[3] In the *O.T., Oedipus* is seen at the outset as fully endowed with the sight of reason, mature, admired, independent of others, while

---

[3] This notion has been proposed by, among others, S. M. Adams, *Sophocles the Playwright* (Toronto: University of Toronto Press, 1957); plainly, he could have elaborated his conclusions.

others are wholly dependent on him; in the *O.C.*, he is blind, helpless, abominated, reliant on a girl, Antigone. In the former, he has the power to curse the unknown criminal, and is thus nearly divine (confident of Apollo's will), sure of his strength and foresight; in the latter, he must abjectly pray to the Eumenides (chthonian forces) for guidance and help. Next, in the *O.T.*, he is the self-assured king in search of the murderer of Laius, and after that, in quest of his own identity. In the *O.C.*, he is the quarry of a quest by others, by Creon and Polyneices, who no more know him for what he is, than he knew the unknown assassin, in the earlier play, for what (or who) he was then. Oedipus did not understand the power of the forces he confronted in the *O.T.*, while Creon and Polyneices show no real comprehension of the power now embodied in the old blind man whom they hope to enlist in their services. The physical blinding of the king in the earlier play coincides with the awakening of his spiritual vision into reality, and he turns to reliance on his daughter and his stick; in the *O.C.*, the old beggar (now like Teiresias) gently pushes his daughter Antigone aside, and with his eyes opened to fuller reality, leads Theseus to the holy place where no others can follow. Finally, at the end of the *O.T.*, he enters the palace, the proper secular dominion in which his birthright lay. But in the *O.C.*, he is mysteriously accepted into the grove of the Eumenides, his sacred birthright, and transfigured by the extraordinary powers of the earth, here to be granted the sanctified and universal hospitality which Sophocles thought the reward of the exceptional sufferer. And for the poet, the exceptional sufferer is man.

The riddle of the Sphinx is close to the heart of both plays. In the *O.T.*, Oedipus re-enacts the riddle; as infant on the slopes of Kithaeron, as the kind and intelligent king at the beginning of the tragedy, as the faltering blind man at the end. The *O.C.* reverses this motif as well. Decrepit helplessness in the opening scenes, the flash-back to infancy, the assured domination and confidence at the end. I doubt that we can regard this inversion of structure as an effect drawn solely by the magnet of appealing possibilities of plot. It is more tempting to suppose that the much older Sophocles, knowing that burial would soon unite him with his fellow-townsman, Oedipus, looked back to the *Tyrannus* and found it wanting—

but in meaning, not structure. It had presented a solution to the Sphinx's riddle, had offered as answer a definition of man. But that definition had been two-dimensional, only *grandeur et misère;* the magnificence of reason, and mortal frailty. The lacking third dimension is projected, largely by structure, in the final play. It resides in the mystically felt and logically undemonstrable spiritual transcendancy of man, the quintessence of his being, not to be found in his confident rationality or in the magnitude of his suffering. Of course the conflict between reason and passion is fundamental to the third and higher characteristic, and leads up to it by a dialectic stated dramatically in the *O.C.* But the *O.T.* had failed to make fully clear this ultimate synthesis of the basic and paradoxical elements of his nature.

By the conscious reversal of structure in the *Oedipus at Colonus,* Sophocles shows us that he was not merely playing a clever formal game, or creating virtuoso variations on a theme of his earlier years. Rather the structural inversion points to a deep rethinking of serious ethical, even metaphysical attitudes. As critics we may not share those attitudes, we may possibly think them shallow, we may find them to be not much more than commonplaces of the Athenian tradition. But however we may evaluate his thought, we have no license to dismiss it as unintended or inconsequential to the emotive effect of his theater. Structure and thought are inseparable in the seven plays; to stress one element and disregard the other is a decision of Solomon, a dismemberment of the living work of art.

The *Ajax* of Sophocles

by *Bernard M. W. Knox*

The key to an understanding of this harsh and beautiful play
is the great speech in which Ajax debates his course of action and
explores the nature of man's life on earth (646-692). These lines are
so majestic, remote, and mysterious, and at the same time so passionate, dramatic, and complex, that if this were all that had
survived of Sophocles he would still have to be reckoned as one of
the world's greatest poets. They are the point from which this discussion starts and to which it will return, for in the play all the
poetic and thematic threads which make up the stark pattern of the
Ajax start from and run back to this speech. These magnificent,
enigmatic lines, alternately serene and passionate, and placed almost
dead center in the action, offer us the only moment of repose and
reflection in a play which begins in monstrous violence and hatred,
and maintains that atmosphere almost unbroken to the end.

It is a puzzling play. Ever since scholars started to work on it, it
has been criticized as faulty in structure, and the schoolmasterish
remarks of the ancient scholiast on this point have often been
echoed, though in more elegant and conciliatory terms, in the
writings of modern critics. Apart from the structural problem, it
is only too easy for the modern critic and reader to find the
characters repellent: to see in Athena a fiendish divinity, in Ajax a
brutalized warrior, in the Atridae and Teucer undignified wranglers,
and in Odysseus a cold self-seeker.

In recent years a host of new and more sympathetic critics have
tried to rehabilitate the play; most influential among them is
H. D. F. Kitto, who, working on the unassailable basis that Sophocles
knew more about dramaturgy than both Schlegels and Tycho von
Wilamowitz rolled into one, assumes that the play is a dramatic
success and then attempts to explain why. In his best-known book
(though he has modified the position considerably in his latest
work on the subject) he found the solution of the difficulty in the
importance of Odysseus, which he called the "keystone" of the play.
Kitto's chapter on the *Ajax* is so well written (and so welcome a
relief after the self-satisfied strictures of nineteenth-century critics)
that it is at first reading overwhelmingly persuasive, but when the
reader changes books and gets back to Sophocles, his difficulties
return. For Ajax, dead and alive, imposes his gigantic personality
on every turn of the action, every speech. When he is not speaking himself, he is being talked about; there is only one subject
discussed in this play, whether the speaker is Ajax, Athena, Odysseus, Tecmessa, the messenger, Teucer, Menelaus, or Agamemnon
—and that subject is Ajax. Ajax is on stage in every scene, first
alive, then dead. The rest of the characters follow him wherever
he goes; Odysseus tracks him to his tent, and later Tecmessa and
the chorus follow his tracks to the lonely place on the shore where
he has killed himself. The hero's death, which normally in Attic
tragedy is described by a messenger who accompanies the body
onstage, takes place before our eyes in the *Ajax,* and to make this
possible Sophocles has recourse to the rare and difficult expedient
of changing the scene; when Ajax moves, the whole play follows
after him. Further, as Kitto indeed points out, the poetry of the
play (and it contains some of Sophocles' most magnificent lines)
is all assigned to Ajax. Brutal and limited he may be, but there
can be no doubt that Sophocles saw him as heroic. The lamentations
of Tecmessa, Teucer, and the chorus express our own sense of a
great loss. The tone of the speeches made over his body in the
second half of the play emphasizes the fact that the world is a
smaller, meaner place because of his death. The last half of the play
shows us a world emptied of greatness; all that was great in the
world lies there dead, impaled on that gigantic sword, while
smaller men, with motives both good and bad, dispute over its

burial. The unheroic tone of the end of the play (with its threats
and boasts and personal insults) has often been criticized as an
artistic failure; surely it is deliberate. Nothing else would make us
feel what has happened. A heroic age has passed away, to be
succeeded by one in which action is replaced by argument, stubbornness by compromise, defiance by acceptance. The heroic self-assertion
of an Achilles, an Ajax, will never be seen again; the best this new
world has to offer is the humane and compromising temper of
Odysseus, the worst the ruthless and cynical cruelty of the Atridae.
But nothing like the greatness of the man who lies there dead.

The poetry of the play is in the speeches of Ajax, and there is
one speech of Ajax which is Sophoclean poetry at its greatest.
ἅπανθ᾽ ὁ μακρὸς κἀναρίθμητος χρόνος. . . . "All things long uncounted
time brings forth from obscurity and buries once they have appeared. . . ." The opening lines of the speech raise the problem
which the play as a whole explores: the existence of man in time
and the changes which time brings. It is significant that the *Ajax,*
contrary to Sophoclean practice as we know it from the extant plays,
brings an Olympian god on stage, for the difference between men
and gods is most sharply defined in their relationship to time—
mortality and immortality are conditions of subjection to and
independence of time.

This difference between man and the gods, the transitory and
the permanent, is a theme which Sophocles returns to in his last
play, where Oedipus, at Colonus, spells out for Theseus what the
difference is. "Dearest son of Aegeus, only for the gods is there no
old age or death. Everything else is confounded by all-powerful
time." He goes on to describe the changes which time brings to all
things human in terms strikingly reminiscent of lines written many
years before, in the *Ajax.* The theme of man, the gods, and time
is from first to last one of the main concerns of Sophoclean tragedy.

In the *Ajax* this theme is developed through the exploration of
one particular aspect of human activity, the working of an ethical
code. This code was already a very old one in the fifth century B.C.,
and although more appropriate to the conditions of a heroic society,
it was still recognized in democratic Athens as a valid guide to
conduct. Τοὺς μὲν φίλους εὖ ποιεῖν, τοὺς δ᾽ ἐχθροὺς κακῶς—to help your
friends and harm your enemies. A simple, practical, natural rule.

From the point of view of a Christian society it is a crude and cynical rule, but for all that it is often followed. But whereas we today pay at least lip service to a higher ideal of conduct, the fifth-century Athenian accepted this simple code as a valid morality. It was a very old rule (a strong point in its favor for a people in whose language the word νέος, "new," had a "collateral notion of *unexpected, strange, untoward, evil*"); it seemed like sound common sense; and it had the authority of the poets, who were, for fifth-century Athens, the recognized formulators of ethical principles, the acknowledged legislators.

Plato's Socrates, who begins the great argument of the *Republic* by rejecting this formula as a definition of justice, denies that the poets could have said any such thing. "We shall fight them, you and I together," he says to Polemarchus, "—anyone who says that Simonides or Bias or Pittacus or any other of the wise and blessed men said it. . . . Do you know whose saying I think this is, that justice consists of helping your friends and harming your enemies? I think it is a saying of Periander, or Perdiccas, or Xerxes or Ismenias the Theban or some other such man . . ."

Plato, of course, when he tries to make this saying the exclusive property of a bloodthirsty Corinthian tyrant, a Macedonian barbarian, a Persian despot, or a Theban intriguer, is writing with his tongue in his cheek. For the maxim "Help your friends, harm your enemies" stares out at us from the pages of the poets. It is to be found in Archilochus, in Solon, in Theognis, in Pindar, and was attributed to Simonides. It continued to be a rule of conduct universally accepted and admired in spite of Plato's rejection of it, and something very like it is rejected by Christ in the first century A.D.: "Ye have heard that it hath been said, Thou shalt love thy neighbor and hate thine enemy. But I say unto you, love your enemies."

This is of course *our* ideal of conduct, the ideal to which, in our better moments, most of us try to rise. Even if, regrettably, we continue to live by the old rule, we have the vision of a higher ideal. But this was not the case in the Athens of Sophocles. The simple formula, "Help your friend, harm your enemies," was generally accepted, not just as hardheaded practical advice, but as a moral principle, a definition of justice, a formulation of the *arete,* the specific excellence, of man.

The *Ajax* of Sophocles examines the working of this code. It is a theme which springs naturally from the figure of Ajax as Sophocles found it already formed in saga and drama, the figure of a man of fierce impulse and action, whose hate for his enemies led him to attempt a monstrous act of violence and, when it failed, to kill himself.

Sophocles' treatment of this theme, however, reveals an attitude which differs from that of Christ and of Plato. It is thoroughly Sophoclean and fifth-century; that is to say, it is at once intellectual and practical, and at the same time ironic and tragic. Christ's rejection of the way of the world (and the interpretation of the Mosaic law which was used to support it) is justified by a summons to a higher morality: "Love thine enemy. If ye love them which love you, what reward have ye?" Plato's rejection of the ancient maxim is based on its inadequacy as a definition of justice: the enemy you harm may be a just man, and in any case, even if he is unjust, harming him will only make him more so. But the Sophoclean presentation of the old code in action makes the comparatively simple point that it is unworkable. The objective may be good, but in the world in which we live, it is unattainable. The old morality is exposed as a failure in practice.

Τοὺς μὲν φίλους εὖ ποιεῖν, to do good to your friends—no one objects to that (though Christ rejects it as not enough); it is the other half of the commandment, τοὺς ἐχθροὺς κακῶς, that raises problems. "To harm your enemies": this accepts and justifies hatred. The *Ajax* is full of hatred and enmity. The hatred of Ajax for Odysseus was proverbial; it is immortalized in one of the greatest passages of the *Odyssey,* and in Sophocles' play it is given full expression, together with his hatred for the Atridae, their hatred for him, and the hatred between them and Teucer. No other play of Sophocles contains so many bitter speeches; Ajax dies cursing his enemies (and his curses are repeated by Teucer at the end of the play), and after his death the venomous disputes between the Atridae and Teucer make the last half of the play a noisy, scurrilous quarrel to which only the last-minute intervention of Odysseus restores some measure of dig-

nity. The Greek words for enmity and hate (and there are many of
them, with a great range of subtle distinctions) dominate the vocabulary of the play. "I see you," says Athena, addressing Odysseus, in
the first lines of the play, "I see you always hunting for some occasion against your enemies." This prologue sets before us, with brilliant dramatic economy, three attitudes toward the traditional code,
and, as is to be expected of the superb dramaturgy of Sophocles,
they are not described but expressed in action.

The simplest attitude is that of Ajax, who has lived in this faith
and is shortly to die in it. He represents the savagery of "harm
your enemies" in an extreme form; he glories in the violence he is
dispensing to the animals he takes for his enemies. He believes that
he has killed the sons of Atreus, and is proud of it; he relishes in
advance the pleasure he will feel in whipping Odysseus before killing him. When Athena urges him to spare the torture, he tells her
sharply to go about her own business. He goes back to his butcher's
work with evident gusto: χωρῶ πρὸς ἔργον—"Back to work" (116).

He is mad, of course, and the madness has been inflicted on him
by Athena. But it consists only in his mistaking animals for men;
the madness affects his vision more than his mind. All the verbs used
by Athena make it clear that she is not producing the intention to
murder the Achaean kings; she merely diverts, hinders, checks, limits, and encourages a force already in motion. The intent to torture
and murder was present in Ajax sane; when he recovers from his de-
lusions his only regret is that his victims were sheep instead of men,
his disgrace is that he failed in his murderous attempt. Ajax did
not need to be driven mad to attempt to harm his enemies; once restored to sanity he never for a moment doubts that his attempt was
justified. We learn later from Tecmessa that he laughed loudly in
the midst of his cruelties. This enjoyment of the shame and helplessness of his enemies is, of course, according to the old morality,
his right and privilege. If it is right to harm your enemies, there is
no reason why you should not enjoy it. There is in fact every reason
why you should.

There is a goddess on stage throughout this scene, and in her we
are shown a divine attitude to the traditional morality. It is exactly
the same, point for point, as that of Ajax. Τοὺς ἐχθροὺς κακῶς. Ajax
is her enemy. As we learn later in the play, he has angered her by

an insulting and contemptuous reply. She harms her enemy. She
exposes him in his madness before his adversary Odysseus, and lets
him convict himself out of his own mouth. Athena mocks Ajax as
he mocks *his* enemies, calling herself his "ally" and ironically accepting his insulting commands. She harms and mocks her enemy, Ajax,
and helps her friend, Odysseus, who in this scene emphasizes his
devotion to her and is assured by the goddess of her continued favor.
Athena is the traditional morality personified, in all its fierce sim-
plicity.

The third figure on stage during the prologue, Odysseus, has come
hunting his enemy. He is told by the goddess that Ajax intended
to kill him, and then he hears Ajax insist on torturing the animal
he takes to be Odysseus himself. Odysseus is given the mandate to
inform the Achaeans of Ajax's criminal intentions, and so becomes
the instrument of his enemy's fall. And he is invited by the goddess
to rejoice in his enemy's disaster, to mock, to echo Ajax's laughter
at the imagined sufferings of his enemies. Odysseus has every reason
in the world to rejoice at the spectacle revealed to him by Athena,
but he cannot do it. "I pity him," he says, "although he is my
enemy." The authority of the ancient heroic code and the explicit
invitation of the goddess both fail, overwhelmed by this sudden feeling of pity. Odysseus abandons the traditional morality at the moment of victory and exultation. He does so because he puts himself,
in imagination, in his enemy's place, "considering not so much his
case as my own," to use his own words. In the ruin of Ajax he sees,
beyond the fall of a man who was, and still is, his most dangerous
enemy, a proof of the feeble and transitory condition of all men,
himself included. "All of us who live are images, or weightless shadows." That the great Ajax has been reduced to this state of deluded
impotence is no occasion for triumph for a fellow man, but rather
a melancholy reminder of the instability and tragic frailty of all
things human.

Of these three attitudes to the traditional morality the most disturbing for the modern reader is that of the goddess. The audience
in the theater of Dionysos had seen gods on stage before, but, as
far as we can tell, they had seen nothing as vengeful and fierce as
this Athena since Aeschylus put the Eumenides on stage; this Athena
seems to derive from the same concept of divinity as that which

later inspired the Aphrodite and Dionysos of Euripides. Her rigid adherence to the traditional code and the added refinement of mockery of her victim seem all the more repellent by contrast with the enlightened attitude of Odysseus.

But we must remember that for Sophocles and his contemporaries gods and men were not judged by the same standards. The Christian ideal, "Be ye therefore perfect, even as your father in heaven is perfect," would have made little or no sense to a fifth-century Athenian, whose deepest religious conviction would have been most clearly expressed in opposite terms: "Do not act like a god." Sophocles clearly admires the attitude of Odysseus, but we must not therefore assume that he criticizes the attitude of Athena. She is a goddess, and her conduct must be examined in a different light.

Her attitude is consistent. Odysseus, whom she helps and rewards, has always been her friend, and Ajax, whom she thwarts and mocks, is an enemy of fairly long standing. His insulting treatment of the goddess in the prologue is not an erratic phenomenon produced by his madness, for much earlier, in full control of his senses, he had insulted her in exactly the same way and in almost exactly the same words, as the messenger later tells us. By his "dreadful words which should never have been spoken" Ajax provoked the anger of Athena, which she satisfies in the mockery of the opening scene.

But her attitude is not only consistent, it is also just. Ajax deserves punishment not only because of his slaughter of the cattle (the common property of the Achaean army) and the men in charge of them (whom Ajax characteristically never even mentions), but also because the real objectives of his murderous onslaught were the sons of Atreus and Odysseus, the kings and commanders of the army. Athena in the prologue is a minister of justice. Her insistence, against the indignant and repeated protests of Odysseus, on exposing Ajax in his madness before his enemy is not merely vindictive, it is a necessary step in his condemnation. The proof of Ajax's deeper guilt, his intention to murder the kings, must come from his own mouth before a witness. What Athena does is to prevent Ajax, by deluding his vision, from committing the great crime he had planned, and to reveal to Odysseus undeniable proof that the lesser crime he *has* committed would, but for her intervention, have been a slaughter of kings instead of animals. Surely this is the working of justice. The goddess thwarts and mocks her enemy, but it could also be said that she baffles and convicts a wrongdoer. The working of the fierce old code, in the action of the goddess, is the working of justice.

That she takes a merciless delight in his humiliation is, in terms of the accepted morality, natural and right; in theological terms it is at least logical. A strict conception of justice has no place for mercy, which might temper punishment and restrain exact retribution. That Athena, in addition to inflicting full punishment, also takes delight in the wrongdoer's fall is, for our modern Christian sensibility, hard to accept, and yet even the Christian consciousness, shot through as it is with the ideal of mercy, can on occasion feel something similar. In the *Divina Commedia* Dante's savage mockery of the tortured Pope Nicholas is warmly approved by Virgil. And the same *anima naturaliter Christiana* sharply reproves Dante's pity for the grotesquely mutilated prophets. This passage is an interesting parallel to the prologue of the *Ajax*. What excites Dante's pity is "our image so twisted," *la nostra imagine sì torta*—a feeling like Odysseus' sympathy for Ajax "yoked to cruel delusion." Virgil's reproof is harsh and bitter. "Are you still one of the fools, like the rest? Here pity is alive when it is truly dead": *Qui vive la pietà quand' è ben morta.*

Athena's attitude is that of a merciless but just divinity who punishes the wrongdoer. At the same time it is the attitude of the victorious enemy who returns evil for evil and exults in the fall of his opponent. In this respect it is exactly that of Ajax, a point emphasized through the repetition of the same words and sentiments in the speeches of the goddess and the hero. "Is not laughter at one's enemies the kind that gives most pleasure?" Athena asks Odysseus, and Ajax describes an imaginary Odysseus awaiting torture inside the tent as "the prisoner who gives me most pleasure." Athena ironically begs Ajax not to "humiliate" his prisoner, but this is exactly what she is doing to Ajax, as he realizes later: "the strong goddess, daughter of Zeus, humiliates me even to death." In their uncritical adherence to the traditional code and their full exploitation of the harshness it enjoins there is no difference between the goddess and the man.

But this does not constitute, as the modern reader instinctively feels it does (and as it would in Euripides), a criticism of Athena. Rather it is the measure of the heroic presumption of Ajax. He assumes the tone and attitude of a god. And in him this is no recent development. He has always felt and acted like this. When the messenger, later in the play, describes his insulting reply to Athena's encouragement before the battle, he defines the nature of Ajax's pride. Ajax was not "thinking like a man." And he also quotes the words of Calchas, which describe Ajax as one who "born a man by nature, does not think as a man." The tone of Ajax's speeches in the prologue is not the product of his delusion, it is the expression of his nature as it has always been. And that tone is unmistakable. He talks and acts like a god; he assumes not merely equality with Athena, but superiority to her. Athena mockingly recognizes this conception of their relationship by her use of the word "ally" (σύμμαχος) to describe herself; the word in Athenian official parlance (it was the official designation of the subject cities and islands of the empire) suggests inferiority, and it is clear that this is how Ajax regards her. He gives her orders, ἐφίεμαι (112), a strong word which he repeats a few lines later (116), he roughly and insultingly refuses her request for mercy for Odysseus, and when she tells him to do whatever he sees fit, he condescendingly orders her to be just that kind of an ally to him always, that is, a subservient one.

Ajax's assumption of godlike confidence is only an extreme expression of his fierce dedication to the traditional morality. In pursuing the heroic code to the bloodthirsty and megalomaniac extremes the prologue puts before us, he is acting not like a man but like a god. "May Zeus grant me," sang that bitter and vengeful poet Theognis, "to repay my friends who love me and my enemies who now triumph over me, and I would seem to be a god among men." Ajax acts and thinks like a god among men. Like a god he judges, condemns, and executes his enemies, with speed, certainty, and righteous wrath. The gods do indeed act like this, but they can do so because they have knowledge. "Learn," says Athena to Odysseus, "from one who knows." But man is ignorant. "We know nothing clear," says Odysseus. "We are adrift." The same standard of conduct will not be valid for man in his ignorance and gods in their knowledge. What is wrong for one may be right for the other.

For the gods, in fact, the old rule, to help friends and harm enemies, is a proper rule. The proviso that Socrates adds to the rule in the *Republic*—"if our friends are good and our enemies bad"— does hold true for the gods. Athena, in harming her enemy Ajax, is punishing a wrongdoer. And in her closing words she makes a claim to this general identification of friend with good and enemy with bad for the gods as a whole: "The gods love those who are self-controlled, and hate the bad." But no man can make any such claim, to distinguish certainly, as the gods can, between good and bad men. "We know nothing clear, we are adrift."

A man cannot know with certainty whether his friends are good or bad, and so with his enemies. But his ignorance is even more profound. He cannot even know for sure who his friends *are*, and by the same token, he cannot know who his enemies are either. Human relationships (and this is demonstrated by the action of the play) are so unstable, so shifting, that the distinction between friend and enemy does not remain constant. Human life is a flux in which everything is in process of unending change. "One day," says Athena, "brings to their setting and raises up again all human things." The name of the flux in which all things human dissolve and reform is time, χρόνος. "All things long uncounted time brings forth from obscurity and buries once they have appeared. And nothing is beyond expectation." So Ajax tells us, in words which recall those of Athena.

The statement is especially true of relations between man and man, friendship and enmity. In time, friends turn into enemies and enemies into friends. The *Ajax* itself is a bewildering panorama of such changed and changing relationships. Ajax came to Troy as the ally of the sons of Atreus, but he turned into their enemy, and tried to murder them. "We expected," says Menelaus over Ajax's body, "that he would be an ally and friend of the Achaeans, but have found him . . . a more bitter enemy than the Trojans." Tecmessa, a Trojan, an enemy of the Greek invaders, saw her city destroyed by Ajax, and became his prisoner and concubine. Yet she is the only one that truly loves him; the man that destroyed her city and enslaved her is, she says, everything to her—mother, father, country, riches. Ajax and Hector were enemy champions, and fought before the ranks of the assembled armies in single combat; when the light failed, and no decision had been reached, they exchanged gifts, in mutual respect, and parted friends. The sword which Ajax carries as he makes his great speech, on which he is in the end to kill himself, is the sword of Hector, his enemy-friend. Ajax and Odysseus, once comrades in arms and in the embassy to the tent of Achilles, are now the bitterest of enemies. The most striking example of the mutability of human relationships offered by the play is one that Ajax will not live to see: Odysseus, his archenemy, feels pity for him and will fight for him against Agamemnon, to make possible the burial of his body. In human life, which is subject to time, nothing remains stable, least of all friendship and enmity. In such a world, "Help your friend and harm your enemy" is no use as a guide. How can a man help his friends and harm his enemies when they change places so fast?

Ajax comes at last to his moment of unclouded vision, in which he sees the world man lives in as it really is. He explores, for himself and for us, the nature of the ceaseless change which is the pattern of the universe. The famous speech in which he does so has caused a dispute among the critics which is still alive; there are two main schools of thought about it. One believes that the speech is a sincere recantation of stubbornness, a decision to submit to authority, human and divine, and so go on living. The other believes that the speech is a disguised and ambiguous reassertion of the hero's will for death, and though different critics of this majority school differ in their estimates of how much of the speech is sincere and how much not, they are all united on the point that the speech in intended to deceive Tecmessa and the chorus.

The first of these two positions, most recently argued with his customary clarity and eloquence by Sir Maurice Bowra, must face formidable objections. For one thing it presents us with an Ajax who later, off stage and without preparation or explanation, changes his mind on the crucial issue of life or death, and Bowra can justify this only by assuming a fresh access of madness sent by Athena, for which of course there is no evidence in the Sophoclean text. But, more important, this reading of the speech ignores completely the striking fact that the language of Ajax in these lines is that of a man obsessed by the thought of death; the words insistently and emphatically bring our minds back to the theme of death. He will "hide" his sword; time, as he has just told us in a phrase which refers to death, "hides all things once they have appeared," and later

Tecmessa will find the sword of Hector "hidden" in his body. "I shall go to bathe"—πρός τε λουτρά—the word he uses is the regular word used to describe the washing of the corpse before burial, and is so used at the end of the play when Teucer and the chorus prepare to bury Ajax. "Let night and Hades keep it there below," he says of the sword, a phrase with ominous suggestions, for the word κάτω (below) in Sophocles always refers, when it is used in this locative sense, to the dead, the underworld, as it does in Ajax's last speech, where he announces that he will talk "to those below in the house of Hades": ἐν Ἁΐδου τοῖς κάτω (865).

These ominous phrases are typical of the speech as a whole; everywhere in it the language hints, sometimes subtly, sometimes broadly, at death. If the speech is meant to convey a sincere decision to renounce suicide, reconcile himself with his enemies and the gods, and live, it uses strange terms—inept terms, in fact. Even in a lesser artist such an insensitive use of language would be remarkable. In Sophocles it is unthinkable.

Is the speech a *Trugrede,* then? Does Ajax intend to deceive his hearers, masking his unchanged purpose, death, with ambiguous words? There can be no doubt that he does deceive Tecmessa and his sailors; Tecmessa later complains bitterly that she was "cast out from his love and deceived." But does Ajax consciously and deliberately deceive her and the chorus? If so, we are faced with a problem as difficult as that raised by the other point of view—a serious inconsistency of character. The character of Ajax is Achillean; it may be all too easily tempted to extremes of violence, but not to deceit.

Many learned and subtle critics of the play have tried to skirt this difficulty, to present us with an Ajax who deliberately deceives and yet remains the simple direct outspoken hero of the tradition, but they are attempting the impossible. They succeed at best in finding a more complicated and euphemistic formula for the fact that, according to this view, Ajax consciously and deliberately deceives his hearers. And that, as Bowra forcefully (and rightly) points out, is the last thing we can imagine Ajax doing.

Not only does this intent to deceive strike us as uncharacteristic; it also seems insufficiently motivated. Why *should* he deceive his hearers? In the previous scene he made it perfectly clear that he intended to kill himself, announced his decision firmly, refused to argue the matter, and brutally silenced Tecmessa's attempt to dissuade him. Why should he conceal his intention now? The only plausible reason critics have been able to suggest is that he wishes to die alone in peace, and must deceive Tecmessa and the chorus so that he will be allowed to go off alone, unmolested, with his sword. But this, especially when the scene is imagined theatrically, is not really adequate. Would Tecmessa or the all too prudent sailors of the chorus dare oppose the will of this gigantic, imperious, raw-tempered and raw-tongued man who has just come out carrying a naked sword? If he stalked off now announcing that he was going to find a lonely place to kill himself, can we really imagine the chorus and Tecmessa putting any effective resistance in his path? They appealed to him as strongly as they dared in the previous scene, and were roundly told to mind their own business; one thing that emerges clearly from that scene is that Ajax of all men is master in his own house. The idea that he would have to lie in order to escape from Tecmessa and his sailors is one that could never have occurred to Ajax. The intent to deceive is not only uncharacteristic of Ajax, it has no adequate motive in the dramatic circumstances.

All this merely replaces the dilemmas faced by previous critics with another dilemma, which appears to be equally insoluble. If Ajax is not trying to deceive Tecmessa and the chorus, masking an unbroken resolve for death with ambiguous phrases, and if he is not on the other hand trying to tell them, sincerely and without reservations, that he will make his peace with gods and men, and live, then what is he trying to tell them?

There is only one possible answer. He is not trying to tell them anything at all. He is talking to himself. During the first part of his speech he is oblivious of their presence, totally self-absorbed in an attempt to understand not only the nature of the world which has brought him to this pass but also the new feelings which rise in him and prompt him to reconsider his decision for death.

This solution of the difficulty, that the first thirty-nine lines of Ajax's speech are soliloquy and therefore rule out the question of his intentions toward Tecmessa and the chorus, is suggested by an unusual feature of the speech, which has not been given the attention it deserves. The speech comes directly after the closing lines of a choral stasimon, and thus opens the scene. But contrary to usual practice, it plunges abruptly into the philosophical reflections on time, without any form of address to the chorus or Tecmessa. In the theatre of Dionysos the vast size of the auditorium, the distance between even the closest spectators and the actors, and, above all, the masks excluded that play of facial expression which in the modern theater makes clear at once the direction of the actor's remarks; we can see, and do not have to be told, whom the actor is addressing. But the Athenian dramatist (and this was especially true of the opening moments of a new scene) felt obliged to establish firmly, clearly, and at once the relationship between the opening speaker and his dramatic audience. He put the opening speaker in some clear verbal rapport with the other person or persons on the stage or in the orchestra, by means of a choral introduction, a vocative formula, or a verb in the second person. But in this speech there is nothing whatsoever to indicate whom Ajax is talking to, nothing until the fortieth line of the speech.

Such an opening speech is almost unparalleled in Sophoclean tragedy. In fact there is only one parallel. It is in this same play, the *Ajax;* it is the last speech Ajax makes. And here of course the absence of verbal rapport with the others is easy to understand; there *are* no others, not even the chorus. Ajax is alone on stage.

The opening lines of the great speech on time give the impression that Ajax is talking to himself, just as he does later when he *is* alone. And that impression is maintained. For thirty-nine lines there is no indication that he is talking to anyone else, no vocative formula, no verb in the second person. The only reference to anyone on stage, to Tecmessa, is a reference which makes it perfectly clear that at any rate he is not talking to *her*—"by this woman," he says, πρὸς τῆσδε τῆς γυναικός. "I pity her," he goes on, οἰκτίρω δέ νιν— as if she were not there at all. Finally he comes to the end of his reflections. His mind is made up. And now he turns to the others, and the words he uses sound like a formula of transition from private reflection to direct communication. Ἀλλ’ ἀμφὶ μὲν τούτοισιν εὖ σχήσει: "Well, in these matters, it will turn out well." And then, σὺ δὲ, "You"—at last he speaks to Tecmessa.

The speech is not a *Trugrede,* then; the first part of it is *selbstgespräch,* a soliloquy. Ajax is working out his own course of

action with that same furious self-absorption we have already been
shown in the previous scene, where he poured out his laments and
curses unaffected by, hardly hearing, the questions and advice of the
chorus. Here, for the first thirty-nine lines of the speech, he is
oblivious of the presence of anyone else; locked in the prison of his
own passions, he fights his battle with the new feelings and the new
vision of the world which have come to him since he made his
decision to die. Only when at last he sees the nature of the world
and his own best course of action does he recognize the presence
of the others, and give them their orders. In these final lines of his
speech there is no ambiguity; his words are clearly a last will and
testament, a handing over of responsibility. "Tell Teucer, if he
comes, to take care of me, and of you . . ." What else can this mean
but "take care of my body and assume my responsibilities?" Ajax
never in his life asked anyone to take care of him; he was the one,
as Teucer never tires of repeating later in the play, who rescued
others. The harsh frankness of his closing lines surely rules out any
possibility of intention to deceive in the earlier part of the speech;
when he turns to Tecmessa and the chorus to give them their orders
he speaks plainly enough. If they are deceived about his intentions
because they misunderstood the course of the agonized self-commun-
ing through which he found his way to the decision, they have no
one to blame but themselves. Though Tecmessa later complains
with pardonable bitterness that she has been "deceived," the chorus
blames, not Ajax, but itself. "I was completely deaf, ignorant,
careless": ἐγὼ δ' ὁ πάντα κωφός, ὁ πάντ' ἄιδρις κατημέλησα (911-12).

The great speech of Ajax, for most of its length, is not meant for
anyone but himself; since he is a character in a play, that means
that it is meant exclusively for us, the audience. He is not trying to
deceive, but to understand, to understand the nature of the world
which once seemed (and was) so simple, but in which he has now
lost his way, to understand what his place is in this new-found,
complicated world, and to decide on his next step. Ajax, we are
told by the poet Pindar, who loved and admired his memory, was
a man "with no gift of tongue, but stout of heart." In this speech
the man whose hands had always spoken for him finds a tongue,
and it is the tongue of a great poet. The lines in which he reassesses
the world and time and his part in them are the first beam of light

in the darkness of violence and failure which the play has so far imposed on us; in that light we can see in their true dimensions what has already passed, and the greater things still to come.

The speech begins abruptly with a description of the action of time. "All things long uncounted time brings forth from obscurity and buries once they have appeared. And nothing is beyond expectation." This is a world in which anything can happen; in the course of time, things which appeared unconquerable find their master. "The dreadful oath and the heart hard as steel are overcome." These are not random examples. The oath Ajax swore, to be the loyal ally of the Atridae in their fight to recapture Helen, an oath mentioned later on by Teucer, has been broken by his attempt to kill them. And his own heart, hard as steel, has been belatedly softened in the interval since we last saw him announce that it was too late to educate him to new ways, by Tecmessa's appeals. "I pity her," he says, using the same words Odysseus used about him in the prologue. He feels this new compassion undermining his resolve to kill himself, and the discovery that he could be softened, deflected even for a moment from his chosen course by a woman's plea, leads him to understand the nature of the changing world, the uncertainty in which he lives. But the terms in which he expresses these new emotions betray the fact that they are rejected by his deepest instincts; the words which come to his lips to describe his new-found pity reveal that in the very attempt to formulate it he has already left it behind. "I too, who was so dreadfully resolved just now, like iron in the dipping, I have had my edge softened by this woman here." His metaphor is drawn from the sword he carries as he speaks, and the word he uses, ἐθηλύνθην, literally "made effeminate," is a word that Ajax can apply to himself only in contempt. We can see, in the words he uses, the heart harden afresh, the sword regain its edge.

He cuts these disturbing reflections short with a decision to act. Ἀλλ' εἶμι—"I will go . . ." He will go to the meadows by the shore, to bury in the ground the sword of Hector; let night and Hades keep it there below. The words he uses, as we have seen, are heavy with the sound of death; they stem from the deepest springs of his heroic nature. But the lines which follow show that, on the conscious level, he is still deliberating on his proper course. He gives

his reason for wanting to bury the sword: "Since I received this
sword from Hector, my bitterest enemy, I have got no good from
the Argives." He looks back to the duel with Hector and sees the
exchange of gifts as the turning point in his career, the beginning
of his misfortunes. The sword of Hector, in the hands of Ajax,
sought out and came near to killing the Atridae and Odysseus,
Hector's enemies. Ajax now repudiates the gift of Hector: "The
gifts of enemies are no gifts, and bring no good." His present
troubles he now sees as caused by the sword, which, given to him by
an enemy who turned into a friend, is a harsh reminder of the un-
predictability of human relationships, a grim token of the inconstant
shifting allegiances in which Ajax has lost his bearings. The possession of Hector's sword, the sword of the enemy commander and
champion, had marked Ajax out as a man apart and alone among
the Achaeans; it may have been the cause, he seems to feel, of the
jealousy which lost him the arms of Achilles. To bury it might be
seen as a gesture of his willingness to accept again the authority of
the kings. One thing is sure: the sword, and Hector's friendship,
has brought him nothing but disaster. "Therefore" (τοιγὰρ), he goes
on, "I shall in future know how to give in to the gods and show
reverence for the sons of Atreus. They are the rulers, so one must
give in to them . . ." But once again he expresses his new feelings
in words dictated not by the intelligence which has brought him to
this conclusion but by the passion deep inside him which rejects
it. "Give in to the gods and show reverence for the sons of Atreus."
He should have said, as the scholiast points out, "give in to the
sons of Atreus and show reverence for the gods." The terms he
uses are loaded with his passionate obstinacy, they make acceptance
of authority appear harder than it really is, and this indicates his
hardening resolve to refuse. "To show reverence for the sons of
Atreus" is a hyperbolic phrase which presents submission in terms
that Ajax of all men could never accept, and yet it also expresses
a psychological truth. For Ajax, the mildest gesture of submission
is as hard as abject surrender. And the phrase also indicates his
instinctive realization of an objective truth. If he is to make his
peace with the kings whom he tried to murder in their beds, he
will have to renounce all pride, humble himself, and beg for mercy.
These words express at once the nature of the action demanded by

his new conciliatory mood and the psychological and objective impossibility of its fulfillment. The will to surrender is suppressed in the very moment and through the very process of its formulation. "Time," as Ajax told us, "brings things forth from obscurity and buries them once they have appeared."

The magnificent lines which follow, which state the argument for retreat, concession, and change, become, with this significant prologue, a description of the world in which Ajax, now that he has at last recognized its nature, cannot and will not live. "Things dreadful and most headstrong yield before prerogatives . . . Winter which covers the paths with snow makes way for fruitful summer. The weary round of night stands aside for white-horsed day to set the light ablaze. The blast of dreadful winds puts to rest the moaning sea, and all-powerful sleep releases what he has bound, does not keep what he has taken forever." This is the world subject to time. The forces of nature, which govern the physical world, "things dreadful and most headstrong," observe discipline, withdraw, stand aside, to take their place in the pattern of recurring change, which is time. In such a world Ajax too, who is "dreadful and headstrong" like the forces of nature, will have to bend and give way. ἡμεῖς δὲ πῶς οὐ γνωσόμεσθα σωφρονεῖν; "In such a world how shall I not be forced to learn discipline?" Most translations and explanations of that line give us an Ajax who is reconciled (momentarily or ironically) to the necessity of surrender, but that is not what the words mean. The future of γιγνώσκω, wherever it occurs in Sophocles, has a special sense (dictated by the context) of "learn against one's will, learn to one's cost," and so here: "How shall I not be forced to learn" or "learn to my sorrow," rather than Jebb's influential "Must we not learn discretion?" And σωφρονεῖν, to observe discipline, is in the context of this play a harsh word, which like γνωσόμεσθα marks one more stage in the hardening of Ajax's determination to repudiate not the sword of Hector but the world of time and change. It is used throughout the play to describe the attitude proper to a subordinate. Ajax himself uses it when he orders Tecmessa to leave him in peace: "Do not question or examine. It is good to observe discipline," σωφρονεῖν καλόν (586). It is the word which both the Atridae use to describe the attitude they think proper to inferiors. "Without fear," says Menelaus, "no army would

be commanded in a disciplined fashion" (σωφρόνως, 1075). Agamem·
non, telling Teucer that as a barbarian he has no right to speak,
issues this word to recall him to a sense of his inferiority (οὐ
σωφρονήσεις; 1259). And it is the word Athena uses in her announcement that the gods love the "self-controlled" (σώφρονας, 132) and
hate the bad; she is contrasting Odysseus' acceptance of divine
guidance with Ajax's rejection of it. These words, γνωσόμεθα and
σωφρονεῖν, like the use of the word σέβειν, reveal that Ajax's attempt
to formulate the alternative to heroic suicide convinces him of its
impossibility.

In the lines which follow, the description of what the pattern of
eternal change means in the sphere of human relationships, Ajax's
heart has hardened completely for death; the sarcastic contempt of
these lines is unmistakable. "For I have recently come to understand that we must hate our enemy only to the extent permitted
by the thought that we may one day love him, and I shall be disposed to serve and help a friend as one who will not remain my
friend forever." His next words make it clear that this cynical
prospect is for others, not for him. "For to the many, the harbor of
friendship is untrustworthy." A world in which friends and enemies
change places, and the old heroic code of "Harm your enemies,
help your friends" is no sure guide, is no world for Ajax. He breaks
off his absorbed reflection with a phrase that announces the end of
his deliberation: "concerning these things, it will be well." He is
satisfied and resolved on his course of action, and he now at last
addresses Tecmessa and the chorus, for whom he has so far had no
word. It is characteristic of him that when he does speak to them,
it is to give them orders. They are clearly the orders of a man who
is taking his leave and handing over his responsibilities: "Tell
Teucer, if he comes, to take care of me . . ." He needs Teucer now
to save his body from insult, but his reputation, his great name,
he will save himself, by death. "You will soon hear that, unfortunate
though I am now, I am saved." And he stalks off, carrying the
sword of Hector.

This great speech explores the dilemma posed by the changing
nature of human relationships; the heroic code of friendship and
enmity proves useless in a world where friends and enemies change
places, a world in which nothing is permanent. Friendship and

enmity, day and night, summer and winter, sleep and waking, one succeeds the other, and nothing remains forever—ὡς αἰὲν οὐ μενοῦντα. This word αἰεί, "always, forever," and its opposite οὔποτε, "never," are used, not only in Ajax's speech, but throughout the play, to point the contrast between time and eternity, between man's life and divine immortality.

Ἀεί, "always". It is the very first word of the play. "Always," says Athena, "I see you always hunting for some occasion against your enemies." It is true that this has always been typical of Odysseus, but on this occasion, when his enemy is offered up to him, mad and ruined, for his enjoyment, he suddenly and unexpectedly changes, and pities his enemy instead of mocking him. The word "always" is belied by the action of Odysseus. "Nothing is beyond expectation"; he defies expectation, ours and Athena's, deviates from what had seemed a permanent pattern. Ajax too belies the word. Tecmessa describes him weeping when he realizes that he has failed ignominiously in his attempt to kill his enemies. "Cries such as I never heard from him before (ἃς οὔποτ᾽ αὐτοῦ πρόσθεν εἰσήκουσ᾽ ἐγώ, 318) . . . he used to explain that always laments like this were the mark of a cowardly and depressed spirit" (κακοῦ τε καὶ βαρυψύχου γόους/τοιοῦσδ ἀεί ποτ᾽ ἀνδρὸς, 319-20). "Kindness," says Tecmessa to an unrelenting Ajax, "*always* begets kindness" (χάρις χάριν γάρ ἐστιν ἡ τίκτουσ᾽ ἀεί, 522)—she gets no kindness from him. On the lips of Ajax the word is of frequent occurrence; he is obsessed with the idea of permanence. "Here is my command to you," he says to Athena, "*always* to stand by me as an ally . . ." (τοιάνδ᾽ ἀεί μοι σύμμαχον παρεστάναι, 117). Odysseus he sees as "the instrument of evil *always*" (ἀεὶ κακῶν ὄργανον, 379-80). He uses the word twice with hyperbolic exaggeration. "Will Teucer spend eternity on this raiding?" (τὸν εἰσαεὶ . . . χρόνον, 342-43) he asks impatiently, and he commands that his son Eurysaces be taken home to his aged mother "to be her support in old age forever" (γηροβοσκὸς εἰσαεί, 570). In all these cases the context casts an ironic light on the word; it is exposed as inappropriate by the reality. And in the great speech which shows us Ajax wrestling with the problem of man's life in time, he uses the word only with a negative: he speaks of the friend "who will not remain so forever" (αἰὲν οὐ μενοῦντα, 682), and of sleep, which "does not keep forever what he has taken" (οὐδ᾽ ἀεὶ λαβὼν ἔχει, 676).

For human beings, subject to time, the word ἀεί, as Ajax realizes in his speech and as the play demonstrates in one passage after another, has no meaning. There is nothing in human life to which it can properly be applied, except to places—Salamis is "conspicuous to all men always" (πᾶσιν περίφαντος αἰεί, 599). But apart from the fixed unchanging landscape, a permanence to which Ajax turns in salutation in his farewell speech, "always" is the mode of existence not of man but of the gods, θεοὶ αἰὲν ἔχοντες, and it is with them that the word is associated when it means what it says. Ajax's father told him, when he set out for Troy: "Wish to conquer, but to conquer always with the god's help" (σὺν θεῷ δ' ἀεὶ κρατεῖν, 765). Ajax rejected this advice with contempt and claimed that he would "snatch glory apart from them." But he has met defeat. And in his final speech he recognizes the connection between "always" and the gods; he calls on the Erinyes to avenge him, divinities who are "always virgin, always all-seeing (ἀεί τε παρθένους/ἀεί θ' ὁρώσας, 835-36). And when later Teucer tries to explain the complicated process by which Hector and Ajax perished each one through the other's gift, he says: "These things, and all things always, the gods contrive for men" (Τὰ πάντ' ἀεὶ . . . μηχανᾶν θεούς, 1036-37).

Only for the gods do things "remain forever." "There is one race of men," says Pindar in a famous ode, "and one of gods. We breathe both from one mother. But there is a difference between us, in our power; the one is nothing, and for the other the brazen heaven, a sure foundation, remains forever" (ἀσφαλὲς αἰὲν ἕδος μένει οὐρανός). This phrase of Pindar's, ἀσφαλὲς αἰὲν ἕδος, is of course a reminiscence of a famous passage in the *Odyssey*, a description of Olympus, the home of the gods. Athena goes to Olympus, where, they say, is the sure foundation of the gods forever (ἕδος ἀσφαλὲς αἰεί, 6.42). The next lines of the Homeric passage may well have been in Sophocles' mind when he wrote the lines in Ajax's speech which describe the alternations of the seasons. For on Olympus there are no seasons, no change. "It is not shaken by winds, or wet by rain, no snow falls on it, but cloudless air is spread there, a white radiance runs over it." There is no alternation of summer and winter, of night and day, no winds. When Ajax speaks of those conditions which on earth exemplify for man the imperative of change, he is emphasizing the difference between the human condition and the divine. The man who refuses to change, to conform to the pattern of alternation followed by the forces of nature more dreadful and headstrong than he is, is thinking not like a man, οὐ κατ' ἄνθρωπον φρονῶν, but like a god.

In the world of time and change, the world in which human beings act and suffer, nothing remains forever. Permanence, stability, single-mindedness—these are the conditions and qualities of gods, not of men. For man the word ἀεί is an illusion; man's condition is described by other words, words which define the fluctuating, unstable nature of human reality. The verb ἀλασσειν, for example. The night brings a situation different from that of the day (ἐνήλλακται, 208); "a god," says Menelaus, "has reversed the situation" (ἐνήλλαξεν, 1060), and the same speaker, gloating over the death of Ajax which gives him his turn to use violence, sums it all up in a powerful phrase: "these things go by turn and turn about" (ἕρπει παραλλὰξ ταῦτα, 1087). The play is full of gnomic, antithetical lines which stress this theme incessantly: "everyone laughs and weeps, under the dispensation of the god"; "many are friends now and then bitter enemies." And Athena has stated it, in the prologue, as the gods see it: "one day brings to their setting and raises up again all human things."

In such a world human attitudes do not remain fixed; they flow, like water. "The gratitude of one who has been loved flows away," Tecmessa says accusingly to Ajax (ἀπορρεῖ, 523), and Teucer similarly reproaches Agamemnon: "how swiftly among men the memory of gratitude felt to a fellow man flows away, and is proved traitor" (διαρρεῖ, 1267). It is no accident that Ajax, in his last speech, dwells insistently on the fact that the sword on which he intends to throw himself is "set" and "fixed." "There it stands firm" (ἕστηκεν, 815), he says. "It is fixed in the enemy Trojan soil" (πέπηγε, 819). "I fixed it myself" (ἔπηξα, 821). The sword is still fixed in the earth (πηκτὸν, 907) when Tecmessa finds him impaled on it. The repetition of this word (the natural opposite of ῥεῖν, to flow) defines the context of Ajax's suicide. The steady immovable sword on which he kills himself is the one fixed point in a world of which change and movement are the only modes of existence.

The great speech of Ajax defines the world of time which is man's place and illustrates the impracticality of the traditional code. But it does something more. It discusses the plight of man, time's subject, not only in terms of his relation to gods and his private relation to other men, friends and enemies, but also in terms of his relation to the community. The dilemma of Ajax illuminates not only the metaphysical and moral aspects of man's life on earth, but also the political and social.

Ajax is presented to us in this play as the last of the heroes. His death is the death of the old Homeric (and especially Achillean) individual ethos which had for centuries of aristocratic rule served as the dominant ideal of man's nobility and action, but which by the fifth century had been successfully challenged and largely superseded (in spite of its late and magnificent flowering in the poetry of Pindar) by an outlook more suitable to the conditions of the polis, an outlook which reached its most developed form in democratic Athens. Ajax is presented to us throughout in terms of this heroic morality; this is the function of the wealth of Homeric reminiscence which editors have noted in the language of the play. The words used by Ajax and about him recall the epic atmosphere of the heroic age, and since many of these words are spoken by his enemies, we are shown a full critique of the ideal, its greatness and also its limitations.

Ajax is μέγας, "big, great." His whip in the first scene is big, and so are his words; his strength and courage are "the greatest," and for the sailors of the chorus he is one of the "great-souled" men on whose protection lesser men such as themselves depend. But this word can be used by his enemies with a different emphasis; to them he is a "big body"—Agamemnon calls him a "big ox." The great size of his physical frame and of his ambitions makes him a man apart, alone, μόνος. This is a word which is applied to him over and over again—in peace as well as war he is a man alone. He is a man of deeds, ἔργα, not words, and when he does speak he speaks with an unassailable sense of his own superiority; his speech is κόμπος, the unabashed assertion of one's own worth. His courage is described in words which recall the warriors of the *Iliad*: he is valorous, ἄλκιμος, impetuous, θούριος, blazing, αἴθων, stout-hearted, εὐκάρδιος, and terrible, δεινός. His courage and audacity, τόλμη, θράσος, are exercised for a personal objective, fame, κλέος, εὔκλεια, and for the prize of supremacy in battle, ἀριστεῖα, of which he has been deprived by the award of Achilles' arms to Odysseus. These are all qualities of a man who is self-sufficient; he has also the defects of these qualities. He has no sense of responsibility to anyone or anything except his own heroic conception of himself and the need to live up to the great reputation of his father before him. He is stubborn-minded, στερεόφρων, unthinking, ἀφρόνως, ἀφροντίστως, uncalculating, δυσλόγιστος, unadaptable, δυστράπελος, and, a word which is applied to him repeatedly, he is ὠμός, raw, wild, untamed—his nature is that of the wild animal, the figure in which he is seen in the hunting images of the prologue.

Qualities and defects alike mark him as unfit for the type of ordered, cohesive society in which the individual's position is based on consent and cooperation. And this is brought home to us sharply by the presence of Odysseus, who is by nature most adapted to the conditions of life in the polis, the ordered society. All that we hear about Odysseus in the play comes from the lips of his enemies, so that the words which describe the man most adapted to society are all hostile estimates. But the words of Odysseus himself, and still more his actions, show us the other side of the coin. As in the case of Ajax and the heroic ideal, we are shown both the qualities and the defects of the Odyssean ideal.

Odysseus is willing to take direction from the goddess. "In all things," he says to her, "I am steered by your hand, as in the past so in the future." There could be no clearer contrast with the unruliness of Ajax, as we see it in the prologue and hear of it later from the messenger. Ajax sums up this capacity of Odysseus to take direction in a contemptuous phrase: Odysseus, he says, is "the instrument of evil always." The chorus sees Odysseus as a man of words; "shaping whispered words, he persuades," and his lies are "persuasive." Persuasion is of course the normal mode of operation for a man in an ordered and lawful society, and in the last scene of the play, where Odysseus persuades Agamemnon to allow burial for Ajax's body, we see this "persuasion" in a different and better light. To Ajax, Odysseus is a man who "would do anything," a man "who will put up with much," πολύτλας (a recurrent phrase used about Ajax by his friends is that he "would not have put up with . . . ." οὐκ ἂν ἔτλη). But here again, in the last scene of the play we are shown another side of this tolerance; Odysseus will indeed "do anything"—he will go so far as to pity his enemy in distress and earn Agamemnon's contemptuous rebuke by fighting for that enemy's right to honorable burial. But it is only to be expected that Ajax should see all these qualities of Odysseus as defects, for he despises and rejects the conditions of human society in which they are the highest virtues.

Ajax, like Achilles before him, is a law unto himself; his ideal is the Homeric one: "always to be best, and superior to the others." The virtues demanded of a man in a society of equals—tolerance, adaptability, persuasiveness—have no place in his make-up. In fact, the situation in which he finds himself at the beginning of the play is a result of his defiance of the community; he has reacted with violence against the decision of the judges who awarded the prize for bravery, the arms of Achilles, not to him but to his enemy Odysseus. Sophocles does not elaborate on the nature of the tribunal which made this award, but he describes it in terms which clearly associate it with the court of law as the fifth-century Athenian audience knew it: the words δικασταῖς (1136), ψηφίζειν (449), and κριταῖς (1243) do not occur in any other Sophoclean play, and they are all words which conjure up the atmosphere of the contemporary Athenian court.

But Ajax recognizes no such communal authority. He sees things always in terms of individuals; for him the award of the arms of Achilles to Odysseus is the work of the Atridae, who "procured" (ἔπραξαν, 446) them for the man who "would do anything." If he had had his way, he says, they would never have lived to "vote such a judgment against any other man." If Achilles had been alive to award the armor (again he sees it purely in terms of personalities), there would have been no question; "no one else would have seized (ἔμαρψεν, 444) them but me"—the word betrays his natural violence and his utter incapacity to understand what the concept of communal decision means.

And yet, in this claim, he is surely right. Achilles *would* have recognized a kindred spirit. More, he would have recognized the truth that Ajax is the greatest of the Achaean warriors after him, a truth which Odysseus himself states at the end of the play, thereby admitting that the tribunal which awarded him the arms made the wrong decision. It is no accident that Ajax, in the later fifth-century tradition, is the great prototype of the simple heroic man caught in the snares of the legal process; he appears in this context not only in Pindar, but also in Plato's *Apology of Socrates,* where, together with Palamedes (another opponent of Odysseus), he is described as "one of the men of old who met his death through an unjust judgment."

But the decision was to be expected. The appointment of a tribunal to award the armor of Achilles is a mythic event which marks the passing of the heroic age, the age which Achilles dominated while he lived, an age of fiercely independent, undisciplined, individual heroism. The rewards life has to offer will no longer be fought for and seized by the strongest, whose authority is his might, but will be assigned by the community. And once the decision is taken out of the hands of the individual and entrusted to a representative body, it is inevitable that the man most fitted to shine in courts and assemblies, to persuade, to yield at the right time, to control his feelings, to intrigue, to "do anything," will triumph over the man who lives by imposing his will on his fellow men and on circumstances by the sheer force of his heroic nature.

This political and social context of the dilemma of Ajax lies behind an important section of his great speech. His vision of the world as a pattern of change and concession, exemplified in the disciplined succession of the seasons, starts from and returns to the phenomenon of change in the relationship between man and man. And as is to be expected of an Attic dramatist writing in the fifth century B.C., this relationship is described in terms which recall Athenian democratic procedure. This part of Ajax's speech is full of words which for the audience were of contemporary significance. The Atridae, Ajax says (668ff.), are rulers, so one must give in to them: ἄρχοντές εἰσιν ὥσθ' ὑπεικτέον. This use of the participle ἄρχοντες as a noun occurs only here in Sophocles, and is of course the usual word for the Athenian magistrates. The lines which follow, with their description of the orderly succession of the seasons, of night and day, reinforce the point, for the archons did not remain permanently in office, but yielded annually to their successors. This implied comparison explains the appearance of the unexpected word τιμαῖς in v. 670—a word which suggests the meanings "dignities, prerogatives, office." Things dreadful and most headstrong yield to authority, to office. A few lines later "the weary circle of night *resigns* in favor of white-horsed day," for ἐξίσταται is a word frequently used of resignation, withdrawal, in a political context.

Ajax's new vision of change in the natural world is expressed in terms that point to the operation of change and alternation in human society; these terms prepare our minds for what follows—his scathing rejection of the parallel phenomenon in human relations. "We must hate our enemy as one we will one day love, and I shall be disposed to serve and help a friend as one who will not remain so forever." It was notorious that in democratic states men changed sides (and with them friends and enemies) fast and lightly; later in the play Agamemnon describes this adaptability, shown by Odysseus, with the word ἔμπληκτος, "mobile, capricious"—the word Thucydides uses to characterize the swift shifting of allegiances in the bloody troubles at Corcyra. The audience which heard Ajax speak these words had no doubt about his attitude to this mobility, for he was echoing a saying of Bias of Priene, which they all knew: "Love as if you would one day hate. For most people are bad." Ajax goes on to complete the quotation, and makes it clear that this cynical prospect is not for him. But Sophocles, by a seemingly insignificant change in the wording of the old saw, made it contemporary and pointed: "For, to the many, the harbor of friendship is untrustworthy." "To the many," τοῖς πολλοῖσι—this phrase, unexampled elsewhere in Sophocles, is a cliché of Athenian democratic language, and puts Ajax's contemptuous refusal to live as other men do in terms of the society of Sophocles' own time and place.

Ajax is indeed unfit for the new age, the political institutions which impose rotation and cession of power, which recognize and encourage change. "Unadaptable" (δυστράπελος) the chorus calls him later in the play (914). It is a significant word (and occurs only here in the whole range of Greek tragedy), for it is the opposite of the word Pericles uses in the Thucydidean Funeral Speech to describe one of the key qualities of the Athenian democratic ideal—εὐτράπελος, "adaptable, versatile."

Ajax belongs to a world which for Sophocles and his audience had passed away—an aristocratic, heroic, half-mythic world which had its limitations but also its greatness, a world in which father was like son and nothing ever changed, in which great friendships, and also great hatreds, endured forever.

But in the world as Ajax has at last come to see it, nothing remains forever (ὡς ἀιὲν οὐ μενοῦντα). The man best equipped to live in that world is of course Odysseus. When Ajax makes his contemptuous formulation of the way the πολλοί must live, with a nicely calculated balance of love and hate, he is thinking above all of Odysseus. And the Odysseus of the play uses exactly the language which Ajax, with fierce sarcasm, rejects. "Many are friends now and then turn into bitter enemies," says Odysseus to Agamemnon. "I am ready," he says to Teucer, "to be just as much a friend now as I was an enemy then." Agamemnon calls him "inconstant" (ἔμπληκτοι, 1358) and dismisses his attitude as selfish (1366). But in the circumstances the attitude of Odysseus is noble. His change of sides, his renunciation of hatred for his dead enemy, is magnanimous, and casts a fierce light on the triumphant hatred of the Atridae, who pursue the old morality to its logical and atrocious extreme—the exposure of the enemy's corpse. It is true that Odysseus explains his new attitude throughout in terms of self-interest. "I pity him . . . considering my own case as much as his," he says to Athena. And to Agamemnon's indignant question, "You want me to allow him burial?" he answers, "Yes. For I too shall come to this." "Every man works for himself," says Agamemnon bitterly, and the answer of Odysseus is: "Who else should I work for?" Odysseus does not try, as the Atridae do, to dress his motives up as moral or political principle; he is thinking of himself, and he says so. But it is an enlightened self-interest. It stems from his vision and acceptance of the tragic situation of man, his imprisonment in time and circumstance. "We know nothing sure, we are adrift." "All of us that live are nothing but images, weightless shadows." These lines are the real basis of Odysseus' attitude. The ruin of an enemy, far from being an occasion for joy, is another human defeat, a portent of one's own inevitable fall. The recognition of time imposes a tolerance and restraint which is the mood of the new age, and of Athenian democracy at its best. The individual can no longer blaze like Achilles, a star brighter than all the rest, but must take his place in a community, "observe degree, priority and place, office and custom in all line of order," adapt himself, learn discipline and persuasion, accept the yoke of time and change.

Menelaus and Agamemnon, like Ajax, hold fast to the old morality. They do what Athena does and what Odysseus will not do: they exult in Ajax's fall. They mock his corpse, are ready to trample on it, and intend to prevent its burial. They take full advantage of the circumstances which make them victorious over Ajax. "We couldn't rule him alive," says Menelaus shamelessly, "but we will dead." They accept the old morality, in their hour of triumph, for all it is worth. But their attitude does not stem from an obsession with permanence such as that which holds Ajax in its grip. They talk and act not in terms of heroic constancy, of "always," but in terms of Ajax's great speech of exploration and refusal; like Odysseus, they recognize and accept the world of time and change. But they are incapable of the tragic sense that world demands. Menelaus, like Odysseus, can see himself in his enemy's place. "If one of the gods had not extinguished his attempt on us, *we* would be lying there dead and disgraced," he says over Ajax's body. He understands even more. "These things go by alternation," he says. "Before this *he* was the fiery pride and violence, and now *I* am the one with big thoughts." But from this vision of time's revenges he does not draw the Odyssean conclusion. "I forbid you to bury his body," he goes on.

And Agamemnon shows the same insensibility. "You rashly insult me . . ." he says to Teucer, "in defense of a man who is dead, who is now a shadow." That last word reminds us of Odysseus' description of all human beings—"images or weightless shadows." Agamemnon's words expose his failure to understand the attitude which acceptance of the world's change and flux demands.

The two kings bluntly and brutally enjoy their triumph in the name of the old morality. The ignobility of their attitude is emphasized by the tragic humility of Odysseus, who abandons the traditional code at the moment of victory and exultation, and even more by the stubborn defiance of Ajax, who reaffirms its validity in the moment of defeat.

Odysseus and the Atridae, with different reactions, recognize and accept the lot of man in time. Ajax recognizes it, in fact he is the one who defines it in his famous speech, but he will not accept it. He claims eternity, permanence, the absolute, and if the world

denies him what he asks, he will leave it. His son, after him, is to
be like him: "Lift him up. He will not flinch at the sight of blood
. . . He must be broken like a colt to his father's raw ways, become
like him in his nature. My son, be luckier than your father, but in
everything else, like him." He is speaking in terms of ἀεί, "always."
His son will carry on his personality. So will Teucer, who after
Ajax's death is as intransigent and undaunted as his greater brother.

After the great speech of Ajax, the chorus impulsively concludes
that he has come to terms with the world of change he describes so
eloquently. They repeat his words. "All things great time damps and
fires. I would say that nothing is impossible now that, beyond expectation, Ajax's mind has been changed." But we know that Ajax
worked his way through to a knowledge of the world of time only
to reject it. And we see him for the last time with the sword of his
friend-enemy Hector, its hilt buried in the ground; he makes his
last speech not to men, but to eternal beings and things.

He calls on Zeus to bring Teucer to the defense of his body, on
Hermes to put him to sleep easily, and on the Erinyes, ever-maiden,
ever-seeing, for vengeance—vengeance on the sons of Atreus and on
the whole Achaean army. As the confidence of Odysseus contracts
so that he cannot contemplate the suffering even of his worst enemy
without pity, so the confidence of Ajax widens to include in his
prayer for vengeance all those who unlike him accept the shabby
world of time. He will be absolutely alone. His last words, the address to the sun and the farewell to the landscapes of home and of
Troy, are the words of a man who is already beyond time. "I
address you for the very last time and never afterwards again."
"Never" is as absolute a statement as "always": he used it boastfully
to the goddess once, but now it will not be contradicted by circumstances, belied by time. It lies in his power, and his alone, to make
it true, and in a few moments, with a swift effortless leap, he will
do so. He has left men and time far behind; his final words are
addressed to things eternal, unchanging, timeless. "Daylight, holy
soil of my native Salamis, foundation of my father's hearth, famous
Athens and its people, my kinsmen, streams and rivers of this place,
and the plains of Troy, I address you all—farewell, you who have
kept me alive. This is Ajax's last word to you. All else I have to say,
I shall say to those below, in Hades." He is going, as he said himself,

where he must go. "All-powerful sleep," he said in his great speech, "releases what he has enchained, does not keep forever what he has seized." But Hades does not release those he has taken; death holds them forever. In death Ajax enters the kingdom of "always." His tomb, as the chorus proclaims prophetically while the dispute about his burial is still going on, will be "remembered forever" (ἀείμνηστος, 1166).

The nature of man's life in time, its instability, is recognized by all three parties, Ajax, Odysseus, the Atridae. The only code of conduct proper to such a vision of the human condition is that of Odysseus, a tolerant and tragic humility. Ajax, who stubbornly maintains the old code and its claims for permanence, renounces life. But the Atridae, fully conscious of the instability of all things human, stick by the old code and blindly enjoy their moment of triumph. They condemn themselves out of their own mouths. Their calculating appeals to order, discipline, reasons of state, fail to mask the ignobility of their attitude, which is exposed by the tragic acceptance of Odysseus on the one hand and the tragic defiance of Ajax on the other.

Ajax's defiance of time and its imperative of change consists not in his suicide (which was in any case his only way of escape from ignominious death) but in his final reassertion of hatred, his passionate vindication of the old heroic code. The problem which faces Ajax is not whether to live or to die, for die he must, but in what mood to die. He dies, as he had lived, hating his enemies. He does not know, and we are made to feel that he would not want to know, that his most hated enemy, Odysseus, will champion his cause against the Atridae. He would rather die than have to recognize Odysseus as a friend. He dies to perpetuate his hatred. His last fierce, vengeful, and beautiful speech is an attempt to arrest, for one man at least, the ebb and flow of relationship between man and man; he may be utterly alone, but he at least will hate his enemies forever.

His brother Teucer understands this. That is why he will not let Odysseus take part in the burial of Ajax. Ajax killed himself to defy a world in which he might one day have to help or feel gratitude to Odysseus. "I shrink from letting you put your hands on his body to help bury him. I am afraid it would offend the dead man." Teucer is right, of course. Ajax hates Odysseus more than any other man. And these words of Teucer remind us, as they must have reminded and were doubtless meant to remind the Athenian audience, of Odysseus' own account, in Homer, of his meeting with the shade of Ajax in the lower world: "Only the shade of Ajax . . . stood apart in anger . . . 'Ajax,' I said, 'so you were not going to forget your anger against me, even in death . . . Come here to me, my lord, hear what I have to say. Subdue your pride and noble spirit.' So I spoke to him. He made no answer, but strode off after the other shades to the dark house of the dead and gone." Οἴη . . . νόσφιν ἀφειστήκει κεχολωμένη, alone, apart, in anger. This is the permanence Ajax has chosen. It is an eternity of hatred and loneliness, but it is the permanence he longed for—he will hate always, forgive never. His yearning for the absolute, the permanent, is fulfilled by his everlasting existence as a proud and silent hater of his enemy, alone, but free, free of the shifting pattern of constant change, free of time.

Sophocles' Praise of Man
and the Conflicts of the *Antigone*

by *Charles Paul Segal*

It is no coincidence that the most influential interpretation of the *Antigone*—and one of the most influential interpretations of a Greek tragedy—comes from a philosopher of idealism and dialectics. The *Antigone* is certainly a play of antitheses and conflicts, and this state of conflict is embodied in the presence on stage of two protagonists, each diametrically opposed to the other. Yet as a result of Hegel's famous analysis much discussion of the play has focused on the question of which of the two protagonists has more of "the right" on his side. This approach runs the risk of conceptualizing the protagonists too simply into antithetical "principles" which somehow are, and dialectically must be, ultimately reconciled.

This is not to say that there are not conceptual issues involved in the characters of Creon and Antigone. But the issues are too complex to be satisfactorily reduced to a single antithetical formulation. We must avoid seeing the protagonists as one-dimensional representatives of simple oppositions: right and wrong, reason and emotion, state and individual, or the like. Such oppositions have some validity, but a validity purchased at the price of oversimplification and ultimately a misunderstanding of Sophocles' sense of the tragic. The characters, like the play itself, have many levels which fuse organically, sometimes indistinguishably, into a complex unity; and here the confrontations of the two protagonists create an ever-ramifying interplay between interlocking and expanding issues.

"Sophocles' Praise of Man and the Conflicts of the *Antigone*" by Charles Paul Segal. From *Arion*, III, No. 2 (Summer 1964), pp. 46-66. Copyright © 1964 by *Arion*. Reprinted by permission of *Arion*. Revised by the author for this volume, and notes omitted, by permission.

It is the essence and the marvel of works of the Classical period that concrete and generic so perfectly meet and unite. In this quality Sophocles is pre-eminent. In the *Antigone* the characters *are* the issues, and the issues the characters. But the characters are not only "issues." They are individuals moving as all men do in a complex entanglement of will and circumstance, passion and altruism, guilt and innocence. Their searching, suffering, growth to understanding, and death give to the "philosophical" issues substance and the breath of life. Hence they can move us with a statement that does not falsify the intertwining of idea with particular, concept with action, loss with attainment, that forms the structure of our reality.

Recent critics, abandoning the simple thesis-antithesis opposition and looking at the play in terms of the action itself, have made it clear that it is hard to find much pure "right" on Creon's side, though this is not to say that his fate entirely lacks a tragic dimension or that the conflict is settled merely by a kind of moral default. Antigone, on the other hand, is vindicated by the end of the play, but only at the cost of tremendous suffering, her own and that of those closest to her. Indeed, since she disappears a little after the half-way point of the drama, one may wonder whether it is not the gods, Teiresias, and the rights of the corpse, which are vindicated rather than Antigone herself.

But Antigone and Creon are clearly the central focus of the play. Yet together they give the play a double focus. The "double center of gravity" in the work, as one critic has called it, creates a tension and richness which makes it possible for the action to reflect back upon itself in complex ways. And, as another critic has aptly pointed out, the decisive quality of the moral judgment expressed at the end of the tragedy requires a movement in which there can be sufficient complexity to make the play an adequate artistic expression of the complexity which exists in life.

The complexity lies in part in the fact that the two protagonists, though totally opposed in their views, are nevertheless each bound to the other, "demonically bound," as Reinhardt has put it. Each is necessary to define the other. On the one hand, as Whitman has well remarked, "Antigone is the balance in which Creon is weighed, and found wanting"; on the other, Antigone's harshness would make no sense without Creon's authoritarian willfulness. It is the essence of the tragedy that the one figure seems to generate the other, that the two coexist as complementary parts of a whole. This whole is not necessarily a Hegelian "synthesis" of two opposing "spiritual substances," but something both infinitely simpler and infinitely more complex, something which is antecedent to and more basic than the conceptual formulations about spirit and absolutes. It is nothing less than the nature of man, his place in the world, and the possibilities and limitations of his actions. Around these issues and derivative from them revolve the antinomies which have been conceptualized in so many different ways: divine versus human law, individual versus state, religious versus secular, private versus public morality.

The conflict between Creon and Antigone has its starting point in the problems of law and justice. At any rate, the difference is most explicitly formulated in these terms in Antigone's great speech on the divine laws (lines 450ff.), a speech which is both confession and defence, both plea of guilt and self-vindication, almost encomium. Against the limited and relative "decrees" of men she sets the eternal laws of Zeus, the "unwritten laws of the gods." She couples her assertion of these absolute "laws" with her own resolute acceptance of death (460). Thus she begins to extend the conflict outward into issues of wider scope. She chooses the divine command over the human compulsion, and rejects life with its compromises for the absolutes of death. Indeed, in her terms these absolutes are, paradoxically, just the things which "live always" (456-57).

This speech is also the focal point for themes that reverberate throughout the play. Antigone opposes the "decrees" (*kerygmata,* 454) of Creon to the "laws" (*nomima*) of the gods, and thus sharpens the issue of what constitutes "law" (*nomos*). By implication she introduces the distinction between the man-made and the "natural," the artificial and the eternally existent. The two words, "decree" and "law," have been used confusedly and indiscriminately by Creon (see 162, *kerygma;* 177, *nomoi;* 191, *nomoi;* 203, *ekkekeryktai,* etc.); and they now are seen to diverge.

The same divergence occurs with "justice" (*dike*). Antigone here appeals to the "Justice that dwells with the gods below" (451), whereas Creon is later to define the justice of a man solely in rela-

tion to the *polis,* the state, and to identify justice in private life
with that in public life: "For he who is a good man in his domestic
affairs will be shown just in the city too" (662-63). The certainty
of this identification is severely shaken in the following scene,
where the question of justice comes up in the most intimate of
Creon's domestic relations and drives a wedge between "public"
and "private" justice. Creon taunts his son with "going to law"
(in Greek, "being at a case of justice," *dia dikes*) with his father
(742) and is told in reply that he is mistaken in the matter of what
is just (*ta dikaia,* 743). The chorus is to accuse Antigone of having
"fallen against the lofty seat of Justice" (854-55), but will exclaim,
at the end, to Creon, "Alas, you have seen justice late, as it seems"
(1270).

Antigone's unqualified declaration for absolute values thus pre-
cipitates a redefinition of some basic moral and ethical categories.
They do not fit her and have consequently to be remade. She is
"a law to herself" *autonomos,* 821; and, as she is well aware (46off.),
she must pay the price for standing outside the conventional definitions of "law" and "justice." She challenges human law with an
absolute which she backs up with the resolve of her own death, for
this is the fullest assertion she can make of the intensity of her moral
convictions. She can assert what she is only by staking her entire
being, her life. It is by this extreme defense of her beliefs that she
rises to heroic and deeply tragic stature; and, simultaneously, by
the same gesture she makes herself incomprehensible to the other
actors, Creon, Ismene, the chorus. Only Haemon, who, at a lower
level, makes and fulfils a similar resolve to die, comes close to understanding her; and in his final act, affirming himself truly her
betrothed, he is indeed "married" to her in death. Death is the only
possible union of such natures:

> A corpse upon a corpse he lies, the unfortunate,
> having got his marriage portion in Hades' house (1240-41).

In Antigone's speech on the "unwritten laws," emphasis naturally falls upon law and justice, for the setting is a juridical one
and Antigone is, as it were, on trial. But in the close-knit fifth-
century city-state, "law" and "legality" have a far wider range of
application than they would in the more compartmentalized ethics

of modern civilization. For Sophocles and his contemporaries they involve the entire public and private life of the citizen, his relations with the gods and with his fellow-men, and all the responsibilities, moral, political, social, implied in those relations.

A sense of this wider realm of conflict is given in Antigone's repeated use of the word *kerdos,* "profit," "gain," in her great speech (461-64). She counts it "profit" to die before her time (461-62), "For whoever lives amid many woes, as I do, how does not such a one win *profit* in dying" (463-64). "Profit," however, is one of the words used throughout the play to characterize Creon's narrowly rationalistic and materialistic view of human motivation. But in Antigone's mouth it carries exactly the opposite significance: emotion, nonrational (though equally firm) determination that willingly accepts or even seeks self-destruction, not self-advancement.

In the face of Antigone's resistance all of Creon's rationalism breaks down and is helpless. "Who is so foolish as to love to die" the chorus said at the announcement of Creon's decree (220). Yet Antigone exults in her "foolishness" and turns the word back upon her judge: "But if I now seem to you to be engaged in foolish deeds, perhaps I am accused of foolishness by one who is foolish himself" (469-70). In the very first scene of the play Antigone has asked to be left to suffer the consequences of her folly (95-96) and her attitude continues to the end. Hers is the woman's emotional resistance to the ordered male reason of the state. And she reinforces her action by the least rationally comprehensible of human acts, the sacrifice of her life. It is not that she acts on unreason, but rather that Creon's kind of reason is inadequate to grasp her motives and her nature. This challenge to Creon's supposed rationalism is to make itself felt even after her disappearance from the stage, for the theme of reason and "intelligence" (*phronein*) dominates the last 350 lines of the play. Creon is to see too late the mistakes of his ill-founded intelligence (*phrenōn dysphronōn hamartēmata,* 1261), and the chorus' admonition about proud words teaching "intelligence" in old age ends the play (1350 ff.).

Given the close interconnections in Greek civilization among all the major aspects of life—intellect, morality, religion—it is natural that this theme of intelligence should be firmly linked to the problem of man's relation to the gods. In Sophoclean tragedy, as in much of Greek thought before and after him, it is primarily the realm of the gods which defines the boundaries of what man can know. Where the one realm ends, the other begins, and to overstep the boundary-line is a dangerous violation of the things that are. It is a matter of "know thyself" generalized to the human condition as a whole. In this play, as in the later *Oedipus Rex,* knowledge, or the presumption of knowledge, reflects the limits of human power and man's responsibilities to the areas of the unknown, the uncontrollable, the sacred.

Thus to return to Antigone's crucial speech, it is significant that in discussing the divine laws, she makes a point of man's not knowing their origin ("and no one *knows* when they appeared," 457). Later in her rapid exchange with Creon she opposes a similar statement of ignorance to his positive assertions about law, right, piety: "Who *knows* if these things are held pure and holy below?" (521). Creon understands nothing of the limits on human power and control. For him to know the ways of men is also to know the ways of the gods; he sees the human realm as exactly coextensive with the divine. He expresses this presumption, with characteristic blindness, in his repeated invocations to Zeus; and these slowly build up in a crescendo of arrogance and disaster.

His first references to Zeus seem "pious" enough, though danger signs are tensely present. He first calls upon Zeus (184) after describing the guilt-stained death of the two brothers (170 ff.) and asks that the god bear witness to his own principle that the state comes before everything (182 ff.). This oath is followed, significantly, by the decree itself, the announcement of a deed which all Greeks would recognize as an unusually cruel and severe punishment, if not an actual violation of accepted religious usage. He next calls upon Zeus in 304 ff., also in an oath and when discussing piety and impiety. Yet here he is not even the calm, assured statesman of the earlier passage; but hot with anger and perhaps fearing for his own position, he threatens the guard with death and worse if he fails to capture the violator of the decree. What gives this passage special point is the flash of impatience and the intolerant jibe at the chorus' "foolishness" and "old age" when they suggest, shortly before (278 ff.) that the burial might be the result of divine intervention. Anger and irreverence both mount in Creon when, shortly after Antigone's great speech, he swears her and Ismene's punishment, "even if she is a sister's child, even if she is closer in blood than any who worships Zeus at the altar of our house" (486-87).

ἀλλ' εἴτ' ἀδελφῆς εἴθ' ὁμαιμονεστέρα
τοῦ παντὸς ἡμῖν Ζηνὸς ἑρκείου κυρεῖ. . . .

Literally, the second line goes, "closer in blood than the whole altar of Zeus Herkeios," (Zeus who stands in the forecourt as the household god.) This statement is outmatched only by his reply to Teiresias, shortly before the tragic reversal:

> You will not cover him in burial, not even if the eagles of Zeus wish to snatch him up and carry him off as food to Zeus' throne (1038-41).

This from the man who first entered with "the gods" on his lips (162). And, a line and a half later he adds, in a characteristic fusion of the "intellectual" and the "religious" themes, "For I *well know* that no man can pollute the gods" (1043-44).

It is, then, not by accident that Antigone begins her great speech with Zeus:

> Creon.   Dared you then to transgress these laws?
> Antigone.   It was not *Zeus* who made these decrees of yours, nor are such the laws that Justice who dwells with the gods below established among men . . . (449 ff.).

Zeus is relevant, of course, because he is the supreme god and, as sky-god, is especially affected by the pollutions involved in the corpse. But as a focal reminder of Creon's *hybris* and, more important, as the fullest single embodiment of the realities of the universe he is the measure of Antigone's dissent and of her heroism.

The gulf between Creon and Antigone thus becomes immense. It is among the ironies of the play that he who talks constantly of "pollution" and "reverence" (*sebas*) understands them only in the narrowest and least reverent way. He who has risked total pollution of the city in exposing Polyneices' corpse will seek to avoid pollution by the limited expedient of burying Antigone alive (773 ff.). (The decree originally demanded death by stoning, 35-36.) It is Antigone, condemned for "impiety" (see *dyssebes,* 514, 516), who is far closer to understanding what piety and the gods mean: "In acting piously I have gained (the charge of) impiety" (*dyssebeian eusebousa,* 924). Her very last words in the play reiterate her claim: "See what I suffer, and from whom, reverencing piety" (942-43). Her piety, as her paradox in 924 makes clear, is not easy nor easily grasped by others, least of all the chorus (see 872), who assert that "self-willed passion" destroyed her (875). Yet it is almost an essential part of Antigone's action that it be not understood, that she stand alone against Creon's socially convenient claims of piety, the easy and popular inconsistencies which all agree upon and follow. It is only the tragic character who sees things through to their logical conclusions, and so dies. Antigone, like Ajax, rejects life as compromise, gives up existence when it ceases to come up to the measure of the heroic self-image. "For you," she tells Ismene shortly after her great speech to Creon, "chose to live, but I to die" (555). Here both Ismene's gentleness and Creon's self-willed rationality are left furthest behind.

It is again among the tragic paradoxes of Antigone's position that she who accepts the absolutes of death has a far fuller sense of the complexities of life. Creon, who lacks a true "reverence" for the gods, the powers beyond human life, also lacks a deep awareness of the complexities within the human realm. Hence he tends to see the world in terms of harshly opposed categories, right and wrong, reason and folly, youth and age, male and female. He scornfully joins old age with foolishness in speaking to the chorus (281) and refuses to listen to his son's advice because he is younger (719 ff., esp. 726-29). Yet his opposition of old and young is later to be turned against him by Teiresias (see 1088 ff.), and he is, in the end, to be "taught" by the young son (see 725-26) who dies, Creon laments, "young with a young fate" (1266).

All these categories imply the relation of superior and inferior, stronger and weaker. This highly structured and aggressive view of the world Creon expresses perhaps most strikingly in repeatedly formulating the conflict between Antigone and himself in terms of the woman trying to conquer the man (see 484, 525, 678, 746, 756). He sees in Antigone a challenge to his whole way of living and his basic attitudes toward the world. And of course he is right, for Antigone's full acceptance of her womanly nature, her absolute valuation of the bonds of blood and affection, is a total denial of Creon's obsessively masculine rationality.

Antigone's acceptance of this womanly obligation stands out the more by contrast with Ismene's rejection of it: "We must consider," Ismene says, "that we were born as women with women's nature, and are not such as to fight with men" (61-62). Ismene feels her womanhood as something negative, as a weakness. Antigone finds in it a source of strength. Ismene capitulates to Creon's view; Antigone resists and finds in her "nature" a potent heroism which cuts across Creon's dichotomizing of things and has its echoes even after her death in the equally womanly, though less significant, death of Eurydice.

It is Antigone's very "nature," even more than her actions, which stands in such challenging opposition to Creon. Thus she concludes her first, and most important, clash with Creon with the pointed line: "It is my nature not to share in hating (*synechthein*), but to share in loving (*symphilein*)" (523). Her words not only answer Creon's charge that Polyneices is an enemy and hence deserving of hate, not love (522), but also expose more of the fundamental differences between the two protagonists. In the conflict over basic terms like "law," "piety," "profit," lies much of the movement of the play. The words for "love" and "hate" used by Creon and Antigone in 522-23 (and throughout the play) have a certain ambiguity. *Echthros*, "enemy," means also personally "hated"; *philos*, "friend," means also an intimately "loved one." Creon simply identifies the two meanings; that is, he identifies "love" as personal and emotional (*philein*) with political agreement (see also, e.g., 187) and "hate" with political enmity. But Antigone's being and her action place into dramatic conflict the question of who deserves "love" and who "hate." Hence at the end of their first encounter Creon answers Antigone's "It is my nature not to share in hating but to share in loving" with one of his characteristic dichotomies of man-woman, superior-inferior: "Go below then and love them, if love them you must; but no woman will rule me while I live" (524-25).

Creon's definition of man by his civic or political relations alone extends to areas other than "love." He can conceive of "honor" only for benefactors of the state (207-10) and angrily rejects any idea that the gods could "honor" a traitor (see 284 ff.). He again presumes that human and divine—or political and religious— values exactly coincide. Antigone, on the other hand, looks at "honor" in terms of what is due to the gods (see 77); and Haemon can find Antigone, a woman and a violator of the ruler's edict, "worthy to gain golden honor" (699).

Yet not merely human relations are involved in the conflict between Creon and Antigone, but basic attitudes toward the whole of existence. It is the first stasimon, the famous ode on man (332 ff.) which marks the first significant expansion of the meaning of the action to this broader level. The ode is not without its ambiguities and ironies, for its praise of man's intellectual achievement is severely qualified in the course of the play. It is preceded, moreover, by several blasts of very non-intellectual anger by Creon; and immediately before, the guard, a simple and conventionally pious man, dilates on the element of "chance" in human life (see 328) and exits with a statement of gratitude to "the gods" (331).

The ode itself is also perhaps not so confident as might at first appear. The adjective which describes man, *deinos,* means not only "wonderful," but also "terrible," "fearful," as several commentators have pointed out. But the greatest ambiguity lies in man himself. Man claims control and domination, yet he cannot control himself, has difficulty in controlling other men, and perhaps cannot even control the natural world. The irony of self-control is pointed up by the word used to describe man's civic and legal "temper" (*orgas,* 356) in the ode, for this word means also "anger" and is so used shortly before in the scene with the guard (*orge,* 280). Similarly the word for "thought" in the ode (*phronema,* 354) signifies also "pride" and has that sense in the ensuing scene with Antigone (see 459), as well as at other crucial points in the play.

There is little question that the ode reflects much of the optimistic rationalism of Sophocles' time: the Sophistic view of man's ability to work creatively upon his environment and the probably Protagorean concept that the state, the *polis,* along with law and justice, is a human creation and perhaps the most important stage in man's assertion of himself over against a hostile or indifferent world. The enumeration of man's cultural advances may itself derive from Sophistic "culture-histories," or at least from the new rationalistic, "anthropological" view of man which treats of human civilization as the result of a gradual slow advance. Similar ideas are already present in Aeschylus' *Prometheus Bound,* written perhaps some twenty years before the *Antigone.*

Though Sophocles draws heavily on these rationalistic views he does not necessarily fully approve them. Through this ode he throws them into the dramatic action of the play and allows them to be weighed in the balance of the tragic outcome. It is not that he denies their validity, for he too is obviously much impressed with the range of human achievement. But he can no longer regard "progress" and a Promethean conquest of nature as having the heroic possibilities which Aeschylus—and perhaps Protagoras—saw in them. Sophocles does not see in reason and technical control simply a source of human freedom, as Aeschylus did, but sees in them too a potential source of human bondage and limitation. And his reflections on this subject are to mature in the *Oedipus Rex,* where, it will be recalled, knowledge and intelligence are by no means unambiguous goods, though they are none the less inseparable parts of man's endowment.

Thus, to come back to the ode on man, when the chorus takes up the creation of law and justice after the praise of man's other achievements they say that men may come "now to good, now to ill." (367) He may be "high in his city" (*hypsipolis*) but also "without city" (*apolis*) should he be led to an act of rashness (*tolma*). His nature then, as this "rashness" or "daring" suggests even here, contains an irrational or violent and destructive potential. Perhaps in this shift of emphasis Sophocles means to suggest that success in the areas of law and justice, the areas which concern relations with other human beings, is more difficult and less certain than control over the lower orders of nature. Though the Sophist Protagoras is probably more optimistic, it is interesting that Sophocles' suggestion of the greater difficulty of law and justice would correspond roughly with Protagoras' emphasis on the difficulty and importance of "justice" and "reverence," the qualities which make it possible for men to unite in cities or societies, in the "myth" which Plato puts in his mouth (*Protagoras* 320c-323a).

This complex connection between control and human relations has also a further significance for *Antigone.* Her womanly "nature," centered on "sharing in love," opposes Creon's attitude of domination which stands apart from the otherness both of men and nature and looks upon them as a potential "enemy" to be subjugated. Thus it is Antigone, the woman—or, perhaps, at another level, the "woman" in him—that Creon must subdue, or, in one of his favorite metaphors, must "yoke." It is interesting in the light of this opposition that when Antigone seeks a heroic exemplar for herself, she invokes the figure of Niobe, a loving mother, but also a human being who is at the same time organically fused with the natural world: she whom "the growth of rock, like intensely winding ivy, subdued" (826-27). Antigone's Niobe belongs both to humanity, with its feelings and sorrows, and to inanimate nature; and she symbolically unites the two realms. Thus the snow and rain are not hostile missiles to be warded off, as in the first stasimon (356 ff.), but are as her own tears which she feels running down the rocky ridges of what is now her face:

> Still, as she wastes, the rain
> and snow companions her.
> Pouring down from her mourning eyes comes the water that
> soaks the stone (828-32, Wyckoff's transl.).

Yet Niobe too, like Antigone, suffered from excessive love and pride; but in her, as in Antigone, loneliness and sorrow are transmuted to a higher plane.

It is significant then that the limitations in Creon's attitudes are borne in upon him not only in the area of his personal relations, but also in language which makes another connection between human relations and the natural world and points toward a view resembling the Niobe-image (though less profound), a view in which man does not dominate nature, but learns from it sympathetically. Hence in urging his father to "yield," Haemon chooses as examples of "yielding" trees that bend in the winter flood rather than straining stiffly against it (712 ff.), and he prefaces his advice with a statement about human "wisdom" (*sophos*, 710), which echoes the praise of "wisdom" in the ode (365).

To yield is exactly what Creon finds most difficult, and there is perhaps a further irony in his statement after the encounter with Teiresias, "To yield is terrible (*deinon*), but to resist and strike my

proud spirt with disaster stands also in (the realm of) the terrible
(*deinon*)" (1096-97). Thus when forced by confrontation with the
uncontrollable to "yield," he echoes the lead-word in the earlier
praise of man's power of control: "Many are the wonders (terrors,
deina), and nothing more wonderful (terrible, *deinon*) than man."

Antigone, who in her own way also refuses to "yield," images
more fully the greatness of man. But this greatness is measured
also against Creon's limitations. The contrast between the two kinds
of not "yielding" is well exemplified in the single, concentrated line
with which Antigone cuts through Creon's long rant of 473-496:
"Do you want anything more than my capture and death?" (497).

The scene with Haemon which follows and first explicitly introduces the "yielding" motif brings out more fully the limitations
of Creon's strength. Though Creon spoke for his son's feelings in
the previous scene (see 569 ff.), he nevertheless fears to encounter in
Haemon the same emotional temper and spirit of resistance which
he found in his betrothed. He indicates his fears in opening the
interview with the question, ". . . Are you here *raging* at your
father . . . ?", thus applying to Haemon the same verb that he
used of the two women earlier (*lyssainōn*, 633; see *lyssōsan*, 492;
the word itself is not common and occurs only in these two places
in the play and, indeed, only twice more in the extant plays). The
verb is expressive not only of the way in which Creon regards
those who oppose him, but also of the areas where he feels himself
most exposed and most uncertain. He is obviously reassured at
Haemon's, "Father, I am yours," the first words which his son, wisely,
chooses to utter (635); and he expresses his relief in the expansive
speech which follows (639-680), full of his favorite commonplaces
about rule and authority.

In another way too the scene suggests that Creon's position is
perhaps not so unshakeably firm as might appear. It reveals that
Creon in fact relies heavily on the support of others, whether his
son or the chorus. He cannot brook disagreement. He cannot, like
Antigone, stand alone. And those who disagree he will coerce into
agreement. At the same time he lacks the calm definiteness of
Antigone, and is actually far less reasonable than the "raging"
womanly natures he insults. Indeed, nothing perhaps better illustrates the instability of his supposedly "rational" and consistent

views than his treatment of Haemon here. Reconciliation and praise in the first part of the scene are followed not only by sharp insults in the second, but even by the cruel threat to have Antigone put to death in her "bridegroom's" very presence (760-61). In these sudden shifts of mood Creon undermines the "rational" bases of his action on which rests, in part, his authority. But also he, the ruler, the man of consistent policy, indicates an increasing qualification of the image of man in the first stasimon as the reasoning being, the artificer whose intelligence is shown in the cities he creates and rules.

Another qualification of this ode comes to center on Antigone. The ode included the catching of birds as one of man's triumphs. From the beginning of the play, however, the birds battening on the exposed corpse are the sinister reminders of Creon's authority (see, e.g., 29 ff.), and hence also of his subordination of religious usage to political decree. Yet it is these birds which carry to Teiresias the warnings about Creon's violation of that to which human control does not pertain. The birds too are the subject of an "art" (*techne,* 998), prophecy, which, in its sympathetic listening to the voices of nature stands apart from the more systematic "arts" of control and device (see *to machanoen technas,* 365-66) that man has "taught himself."

It is significant, then, that the guard, in describing Antigone's capture, compares her to a bird lamenting its young: ". . . She raises the sharp cry of lament of a mother-bird in bitter grief, as when, in the empty nest, it sees the bed stripped of its nestlings" (423-25). And a little later the guard speaks of "hunting" Antigone (433). Yet, though he thus connects his action with the imagery of domination in the preceding ode, he has also shown himself capable of a different attitude in the bird-simile, one marked by pity for the hunted creature. At the same time, however, Antigone is the victim and is the one identified with a part of the subjugated natural world (and, as noted earlier, she is herself to deepen this identification in her Niobe-simile, 823 ff.). The guard, though aware and sympathetic, still allows himself to be forced into the position of the "hunter," the controller. Like Ismene, he has good instincts, but lacks the force to carry them through (see esp. 439-40, "But it is my nature to count all other things as less important than my safety"). He fails where Antigone, his prisoner, succeeds; and her success, in death, has effects which create a drastic change in the attitude of the master-hunter, Creon.

The guard's simile not only underlines the sex of Antigone, but also prepares for Creon's far cruder use of the imagery of animal conquest after Antigone's speech (473 ff.), and there too Creon connects conquest of nature with domination of male over female (see 484-85, 525). The parallels sharpen the difference between the guard's pity and the master's unfeeling severity.

Thus it is exactly the womanly element in Antigone which Creon cannot grasp. He must reduce her act to terms analogous to his own in order to understand it, and this he does most clearly in the language in which he voices his suspicions about Ismene (though he means his words to apply to Antigone as well):

φιλεῖ δ' ὁ θυμὸς πρόσθεν ἡρῆσθαι κλοπεὺς
τῶν μηδὲν ὀρθῶς ἐν σκότῳ τεχνωμένων.

The mind of those artfully devising *(technōmenōn)* nothing honest in the dark is wont to be caught beforehand in its thievishness [literally, "as a thief," *klopeus*]. (493-94)

The word "thief" used of Antigone's deed immediately classifies it in Creon's mind with the calculating desire for "gain" *(kerdos)*, one of his favorite concepts. The verb "artfully devising" contains the root *techne*, "device," "craft," which, as already noted, figures prominently in the ode on man. But as the *techne* of the ode on man is answered (in part) by Teiresias' god-directed *techne* of prophecy, so the reduction of Antigone's motives to a narrowly conceived "thief-like" calculation is answered, also by the gods, in Creon's cry when he hears his son's voice close to the end: "Am I deceived, thief-like, by the gods" *(theoisi kleptomai,* 1218).

Thus the themes of the birds, *techne,* male domination over female, are all linked as parts of a single complex, the multiple aspects of control and authority; and in this complex, which involves Antigone's death and the prophetic birds of Teiresias, it is perhaps suggested that the world of nature, to say nothing of the world of man, is neither so helpless nor so easily controllable as the first stasimon might lead one to suppose.

Antigone, as a woman and "hunted" victim, and Teiresias as

interpreter of the signs from the gods and as a helpless, blind old man, are closely related to one another in their attitude of sympathetic relation with this natural world (and the comparison of Antigone to a screaming bird helps reinforce this association). Both have a special reverence for the divine which deeply antagonizes Creon. Both belong to an order of being or a stage of life of which Creon is contemptuous; and yet both in the end are vindicated at Creon's expense.

In putting Antigone to death Creon has indeed gained his object, solidified his authority, crushed the refractory element that opposed—and this was the only element, so far, that opposed. He expected men (see 248, "Who of men (*andrōn*) dared to do this deed") and gain-seeking calculation, and finds instead a girl who seeks her only "gain" in death (461 ff.) and looks to the gods, not to men. Rebellion there is, as he feared, but rebellion against a profounder and more deep-seated aspect of himself and his rule than he yet suspects. It is with the vindication of these "rebellious" areas, the womanly, the divine, the non-rational, that the latter half of the play is largely concerned; and it is perhaps this reason which in part accounts for the increasing prominence of Eros and Dionysos, the mythical embodiments of the least rational or "controllable" elements in human experience, in the odes of the second half of the play.

The answer to Creon, then, is two-fold. In the person of Antigone is revealed Creon's reduction not only of womanly nature, but of human nature in general. In his reply to Antigone's speech on the divine laws Creon uses not only the language of technical control (fire and metallurgy, 474-76) and animal subjugation (the taming of horses, 477-78), but also implicitly compares Antigone to a slave (*doulos*, 479). The progression of the thought is highly significant, for it reveals the link between man's proud conquest of nature and Creon's debasement of man. Antigone's ability to resist the weight of argument and civic authority brought against her is itself a reply, a vindication of the unconquerable dignity and worth of the individual. She replies to the insult of slavery quite specifically, and her answer is the love and devotion of one individual to another under the sanctity of ties that are independent of the "artificial" aspects of the social order. It is the irreducible humanity of her bond, her refusal to let Polyneices become less than what she has felt him to be, that forms the kernel of her terse reply: "It was no slave (*doulos*) but a brother who died" (517).

The other part of the reply to Creon comes from the subdued realm of nature, wherein the gods are most manifest. This answer too is necessary for the wholeness of the play, for Creon has violated not only personal relations, but something in the relation of man to the world, a sense of the sanctity in things, in nature as in man. These realms, the divine and the human, the natural and the divine worlds, fuse in the rapid movement of events which precipitate Creon's disaster. First Teiresias' birds. Then the terrible encounter between Creon and his son. The language used in this latter scene creates an even more decisive and more bitter inversion of the man-nature, human-animal theme. There is here an ironic alternation of tameness and wildness, but fearfully presented at the height of the peripety in Creon's own son. Haemon's voice, Creon cries out, "fawns on me" (σαίνει, 1214); and the verb recalls the terms for animal-like servility both in the ode on man (see 340, 350-52) and in the exchanges between Creon and Antigone (477-78, 509). Immediately after, however, Haemon is like a wild, untamed animal, with "wild (*agriois*) eyes," spitting, and finally turning on himself in his savagery (1231-36). Like an animal too he has lost man's proud achievement of speech (see 354), and seems not to understand his father's words (see 1230).

Creon's brutalization of his human relationships has thus rebounded upon him and with it the "tameness" and obedience he demands from his own environment. Creon pays through his son for a reduction of man which he has previously inflicted on him. He had totally rejected, or refused to see, any possible love between Haemon and Antigone and thus rejected too the human individuality of his son. In the words, "There are other fields for him to plow" (569), he brings the most intimate of human relations, with its traditional sanctities, down to the level of a brutish act and makes a connection too with the attitude in the ode on man (note the emphasis on plowing at the end of the first strophe, 337 ff.). This degradation of the marriage tie continues in Creon's cruel taunt to Haemon that Antigone will die "in the presence of her 'bridegroom' " (760-61) and in Antigone's long, ensuing lament that she is "wedding" Acheron (816) and that her tomb is her "bridal chamber" (891). The pattern is fulfilled in Haemon's "marriage," in death, to Antigone (1240 ff.) with the consequent destruction of Creon's marriage and the son it produced.

Creon thus comes to learn the consequences of his attitudes and actions on two levels, which might be labeled internal and external, the personal realm and the outside world. Internally, through his sufferings in his own most essential relations, those which both define and express what a man is, he learns that one does not devalue the human realm without doing harm to his own humanity. Antigone, with her absolute valuation of human ties, would then express the fullest development of this humanity and in her Niobe-image rises to almost god-like stature. Creon, having demeaned the sanctity of these ties, is left without any, and hence scarcely human, a nonentity, as he says at the end, "existing no more than a nobody," or, as Wyckoff translates, "I who am nothing more than nothing now" (1325).

Externally, through the intervention of the divine powers in the person of Teiresias, Creon learns by coercion that there are areas of existence that cannot or should not be subjected to control and authority. But this compulsion from the realm of the gods and the natural world is at once brought home to him in terms of his own fate, and he is touched by the broader reversals connected with the birds through the animal-imagery of his son's attempted parricide and death. Thus the two realms, internal and external, human world and natural world are inseparably linked, and the play, in its greatness and complexity, is an expression of this unity.

The confounding of tameness and wildness in Haemon's death is connected with an even more fundamental reversal in the play and with another qualification of Creon's views of civilization. This appears in the theme of shelter. In the second scene with the guard which follows the ode on man and is an obvious pendant to the first scene in this symmetrically structured play, the guard dwells on his and his companions' exposure to the elements as they watch the body: the force of the winds, the heat, the open air, the barren hills (410 ff.). The fact that these details come so soon after the ode is significant, for there shelter from storm and the

open air was prominently enumerated among civilized man's
achievements:

$$... δυσαύλων$$
$$πάγων ἐναίθρεια καὶ δύσομβρα φεύγειν βέλη. ...$$

(Statecraft is his,)
And his the skill that deflects the arrows of snow,
the spears of winter rain (356–59, trans Fitts and Fitzgerald)

A literal translation makes the connection a little more explicit:

He has taught himself to flee the missiles of frosts
of the open air (*enaithreia*) that make hard lodging
and the arrows of storm.

The storm described by the guard fills "the open air" (*aither*,
415, 421), and the image of arrows or missiles was used in Creon's
previous angry interview with the guard (241, keeping the reading of the Mss. with Jebb) and is to be used again by him, also in
anger, against Teiresias (1033-34). Creon himself is responsible for
a "storm" of sorts, for the guard begins his second scene with Creon
by describing his first interview in terms of "the storm of your
threats to which I was subject" (391), before going on to the real
storm in 417 ff. Combined with the animal and hunting images in
423 ff. and 433 (see above) the contrast with the ode is impressive.

That these themes of shelter and exposure have also the broader
implications of communal life in general appears from Haemon's
cross-examination of Creon:

Creon. Is not the *polis* considered as belonging to the ruler?
Haemon. You would exercise a good rule alone, over a deserted
(*eremos*) land (739-40).

And something of this suggestion is acted out when, subsequently,
Creon makes Antigone "deserted," "isolated" (*eremos*, 887, 919),
and her cave is in a wild and "deserted" (*eremos*, 773) place.
Thus Creon, for all his praise of "law," has failed to grasp some of
the essential qualities of civilization taken in its broader, more
humane sense; and he appears as reversing, as it were, the process
of civilization itself in exposing man to the desolation and violence of the world he has supposedly conquered.

This "regressive" tendency is present in the fundamental situation of the plot itself, the exposure of a man's body to dogs and birds. In the corpse, as in the storm and in Antigone's cave, we are reminded of the reality of the still untamed wildness which lies outside human civilization. Like the plague in the *Oedipus Rex,* the mouldering corpse, quickly but effectively described (see, e.g. 29-30, 205 f., 410) makes us uncomfortably aware of something disturbing, offensive, nauseating.

In the Greek view, however, these physically offensive elements have a profounder religious significance. They constitute, as Teiresias brings home, a *miasma,* a "pollution," an infectious taint which is the concrete manifestation of a violation of some religious sanction. The exposed corpse is both an outrage of moral sanctions and a source of real "pollution," a possible cause of plague, blight, barrenness, of the outbreak against man of all the uncontrollable and mysterious forces on which his survival depends. When the right relation with these forces is broken, man's very existence is threatened, on the level both of political coherence (see 1080 ff.) and personal happiness (as Creon is to learn).

As leader of the *polis* Creon must be concerned with such pollutions; yet it is only superficially that he grasps the significance of a "pollution" coming from a violation of the divinely established order of things. In his limited concern for the way in which the city will "escape pollution" (776), in the case of Antigone's death and, more markedly, in his hybristic statement about man's not being able to "pollute the gods" (1043 f.) he shows his lack of a sense of the larger sphere of which the *polis,* and every human creation, may be a part. Near the very end, in a final utterance about pollution, he conveys his newly-gained sense of the limitations of human action: "O harbor of Hades, *hard to purify,* why, why do you destroy me" (1284 f.; see also 1142).

Thus the corpse, in its connections with the themes both of shelter and pollution, serves as an active link between the two aspects of Creon's "irreligious" attitude, his degradation of man and his disregard of the divine sanctions. The two themes are linked, of course, in Antigone too, for her burial of Polyneices is both a vindication of the divine sanctions and a more authentic statement of the dignity of man than the assertion of human in-

dependence and control affirmed by Creon. As the presence of
the exposed and animal-torn body makes clear, the purely man-
centered magnification of human achievement may involve, paradoxically, a debasement of man.

It is not that the confidence of the first stasimon is utterly
negated. The image of man's greatness persists throughout the
play, but it persists in the figure of Antigone rather than Creon.
The qualification of the view of man implied in the ode only
works toward a clearer definition of the wholeness of man, the
feminine with the masculine, the weakness and uncertainty which
are always there, even in his most splendid achievements, the
nothingness in the face of which his greatness is asserted. This
greatness, as Sophocles sees it, has not reached its full measure
unless it has confronted its own negation in death. This Antigone
alone does. Death is merely brushed aside in the ode on man
(361-62) and used as a threat of punishment, another instrument of control, by Creon.

Yet here the fates of the two protagonists, Antigone unshakeably firm and accepting death heroically, Creon crushed to "nothingness" (1325), are at extreme polarities. Though the original
positions of strong and weak are reversed, the two are still separated each from the other as by an infinite gulf. In the *Oedipus Rex*
of perhaps a decade later Sophocles' statement about the complex
interplay of human greatness and human weakness will be more
fully unified into a single protagonist. And at the end of his life
he will again use the figure of Oedipus as his prototype of a still
more profound restatement of this complex relation.

The forceful presence of death, whether in the exposed dead
body or in Antigone's acceptance of a living death, sharpens the
problem of the nature and dignity of man. Death can be a degradation or an affirmation of human value in the face of inflexible
necessities. Antigone's death affirms this value not only for herself
but also for the dishonored corpse. For her it is still a human figure,
still inseparable from a human personality. Creon, in maltreating
the corpse, devalues also the image of living man. It is interesting
to consider Creon's act in the light of the heightened emphasis on
the human form in the mid fifth century. Sophocles presents a
play that centers about the desecration of a human body at the

very time that his contemporaries working on the Parthenon were discovering and expressing the beauty and nobility of man's body as it had never been expressed before.

Again, therefore, Creon's act has implications which he himself does not realize. In regarding death as another instrument of control, not as a necessary condition of existence to be approached with compassion and understanding, Creon disvalues his subjects and ultimately himself. He denies that the state has a place for death in this latter, generic sense. Yet at the end he who had imperiously ordered the maltreatment of a body enters himself carrying a corpse, and one that is "not another's" but his own (1257-60). As a king, he has dismissed or "used" death, only to discover and experience it as a man, mortal and tied to mortal beings. Hence Creon's state-centered view of man reveals its inadequacies in widening areas as the play proceeds and is shown to involve the loss of the full humanity not only of the subject citizen, but of the ruler as well.

A political or historical interpretation of a work of the magnitude of the *Antigone* is, of course, inadequate; yet the historical side has some wider ranges of significance. The play, at one level, is almost certainly a statement about the nature and ideals of Athenian democracy. It rejects the autocratic materialism and narrow rationalism implied in Creon's outlook, which restricts man's nature to a functional capacity, reduces him to a member of a political unit only. What Antigone demands, on the other hand, is that the state take into itself the sanctity of blood relations, the value of affection and emotional ties, the uniqueness of the individual. The conception seems not unlike that put forth in Pericles' Funeral Speech:

> It is true that we are called a democracy, for the administration is in the hands of the many and not of the few. But while the law secures equal justice to all alike in their private disputes, the claim of excellence is also recognized; and when a citizen is in any way distinguished, he is preferred to the public service, not as a matter of privilege, but as the reward of merit. (Thucydides, 2.37.1, tr. Jowett.)

In such a state an Antigone could exist—perhaps in a fuller way than Pericles intends—demanding her rights and thereby shaping the state after the best elements in herself, making it an expression of her own full humanity.

It has often been suggested, as noted earlier, that Sophocles intended the play, at least in part, as a qualification of the rational optimism of the fifth-century "enlightment" as expressed in the speculations of Protagoras, Anaxagoras, Democritus, Hippocrates, Hippodamus of Miletus. It may be too, as has been maintained, that behind the picture of Creon lies some reference to the "proud and austere" Pericles himself, "who with all his belief in humanity was so much less 'human' than, for instance, Sophocles."

But the issues go far beyond the reference to specific men or class of men. They are concerned with defining that in which man's humanity consists. Man would like to believe, the play seems to say, that he has developed "wonderful" resources for understanding and commanding his world. Yet man the artificer or deviser is not enough. Thus in the course of the play all the apparent conquests enumerated in the first stasimon prove to have a double edge. The sea, controlled proudly in the ode (335 ff.) and for Creon, from his first appearance, boastfully associated with political control (the ship of state: see 162 ff., 189-90, etc.), returns in subsequent odes in connection with the helplessness of irrational suffering (see 584 ff., 953 ff., 966 ff.), until Creon himself speaks of his disaster, ironically, as a "harbor" (1284). The animals and birds described in the antistrophe (343 ff.) become the messengers of the violated divine order of things and, in the imagery connected with Haemon's death, almost the immediate instruments of Creon's doom. Speech and communication (354) degenerate into ranting and insult or the utter, animal-like silence of Haemon at the end. Shelter and the fruits of man's city-creating temper (see 355-56) are denied the corpse and even the guards who watch it, and are negated also in Antigone's desolate place of burial. Even the conquest of disease (363-64) rebounds on man in the "divine disease" of the storm (425) and, more seriously, in the pollution with which the city "is diseased" as a result of Creon's "thought" or "intelligence" (1015).

It is only death, that alone which man cannot control or "flee," as the ode says (361), which proves the fullest touchstone of man's greatness and the truest means to his assertion of his humanity. The *Antigone* is still bleak and dark by comparison to the sublime

finale of the *Oedipus at Colonus* where the hero discovers his
greatest powers in his self-guided movements at his call to death.
Yet in the *Antigone* too a self-accepted death is the source of what
is beautiful and heroic in the play. But if Antigone, with her heroic
acceptance of the unknown, of death, most fully vindicates the
dignity of man, Creon comes to act out the equally tragic process
of becoming fully human. With Antigone's death there comes,
through the blindness and helplessness of the seer, the rebirth of
Creon's humanity, until he too is plunged amid loss and suffering
into his own experience of the "unwritten laws" which all men
must face as mortal beings who sometime encounter the unknown
and unknowable. And in his encounter he passes from his communal position as head of state to a loneliness and isolation perhaps
more terrible than Antigone's.

Antigone's view, then, for all its idealism, is more "realistic,"
in the full tragic sense, than Creon's. To live humanly, in Sophocles' terms, is to know fully the conditions of man's existence;
and this means to accept the gods who, in their limitless, ageless
power (see 604 ff.) *are* those conditions, the unbending realities
of the universe.

Sophocles never says that to accept the conditions is easy. Yet
he seems also to assert that man not only must accept the conditions, but that he has, or finds, the strength to do so. Even Creon,
though far from the broken but still imperious Oedipus at the
end of the *Tyrannus*, does not kill himself, crushed as he is. He
suffers and endures.

It is in his appreciation of human greatness that Sophocles is
the true contemporary of the statesman who sponsored the new
Acropolis and Parthenon and of the thinker who said that "Man
is the measure of all things." But he is a universal tragic poet in
his deeply felt knowledge that man's human qualities, in all their
greatness, involve recognition of the unyielding factuality of "the
things that are," the gods. The first stasimon is justly described
as a praise of man; but exactly what in man Sophocles is praising
can be seen only in terms of the entire play. In another chorus
the elders sing, "Nothing of magnitude comes into the life of
mortals without suffering and disaster" (613-14).

The Ode on Man
in Sophocles' *Antigone*

by Martin Heidegger

We read the first chorus from the Antigone of Sophocles
(lines 332-75). First we listen to the Greek words in order to get
some of the sound into our ears. The translation runs:

> There is much that is strange, but nothing
> that surpasses man in strangeness.
> He sets sail on the frothing waters
> amid the south winds of winter
> tacking through the mountains
> and furious chasms of the waves.
> He wearies even the noblest
> of the gods, the Earth,
> indestructible and untiring,
> overturning her from year to year,
> driving the plows this way and that
> with horses.
> And man, pondering and plotting,
> snares the light-gliding birds
> and hunts the beasts of the wilderness
> and the native creatures of the sea.
> With guile he overpowers the beast
> that roams the mountains by night as by day,
> he yokes the hirsute neck of the stallion
> and the undaunted bull.

And he has found his way
to the resonance of the word,
and to wind-swift all-understanding,
and to the courage of rule over cities.
He has considered also how to flee
from exposure to the arrows
of unpropitious weather and frost.

Everywhere journeying, inexperienced and without issue,
he comes to nothingness.
Through no flight can he resist
the one assault of death,
even if he has succeeded in cleverly evading
painful sickness.

Clever indeed, mastering
the ways of skill beyond all hope,
he sometimes accomplishes evil,
sometimes achieves brave deeds.
He wends his way between the laws of the earth
and the adjured justice of the gods.
Rising high above his place,
he who for the sake of adventure takes
the nonessent for essent loses
his place in the end.

May such a man never frequent my hearth;
May my mind never share the presumption
of him who does this.

The following commentary is necessarily inadequate, if only because it cannot be built up from the poet's entire work or even
from the whole tragedy. Here I shall not be able to go into the
choice of readings or the changes that have been made in the text.
Our interpretation falls into *three phases,* in each of which we shall
consider the whole poem from a different point of view.

In the first phase we shall set forth the intrinsic meaning of the
poem, that which sustains the edifice of words and rises above it.

In the second phase we pass through the whole sequence of
strophes and antistrophes and delimit the area that is opened up
by the poem.

In the third phase we attempt to take our stand in the center of the poem, with a view to judging who man is according to this poetic discourse.

First phase. We seek that which sustains the whole and towers above it. Actually we have not far to seek. It is threefold; it bursts upon us like a triple assault, shattering at the very outset all every-day standards of questioning and definition.

The first is the beginning:

> There is much that is strange, but nothing
> that surpasses man in strangeness.

In these first two verses the poet anticipates. He will spend the rest of the poem in catching up with himself. Man, in *one* word, is *deinotaton,* the strangest. This one word encompasses the extreme limits and abrupt abysses of his being. This aspect of the ultimate and abysmal can never be discerned through the mere description that establishes data, even though thousands of eyes should examine man, searching for attributes and states. Such being is disclosed only to poetic insight. We find no portrayal of exist-ing specimens of man; nor do we find any sort of blind and fatuous inflation of human essence from below, inspired by peevish yearn-ing for some unattained glory; here there is no suggestion of a pre-eminent personality. Among the Greeks there were no personalities (and for this reason no supra-personality). Man is *to deinotaton,* the strangest of the strange. Here we must anticipate an explana-tion of the Greek word *deinon* and of our translation. This calls for a tacit glance over the whole poem, which alone can provide an appropriate interpretation of the first two verses. The Greek word *deinon* has the strange ambiguity with which Greek discourse cuts across the contending separations [Aus-einander-setzungen] of being.

On the one hand *deinon* means the terrible, but not in the sense of petty terrors, and above all not in the decadent, insipid, and useless sense that the word has taken on today, in such locu-tions as "terribly cute." The *deinon* is the terrible in the sense of the overpowering power which compels panic fear, true fear; and in equal measure it is the collected, silent awe that vibrates with its own rhythm. The mighty, the overpowering is the essential character of power itself. Where it irrupts, it *can* hold its overpowering power in check. Yet this does not make it more innocuous, but *still* more terrible and remote.

But on the other hand *deinon* means the powerful in the sense of one who uses power, who not only disposes of power [Gewalt] but is violent [gewalt-tätig] insofar as the use of power is the basic trait not only of his action but also of his being-there. Here we use the word violence in an essential sense extending beyond the common usage of the word, as mere arbitrary brutality. In this common usage violence is seen from the standpoint of a realm which draws its standards from conventional compromise and mutual aid, and which accordingly disparages all violence as a disturbance of the peace.

The essent as a whole, seen as power, is the overpowering, *deinon* in the first sense. Man is *deinon,* first because he remains exposed within this overpowering power, because by his essence he belongs to being. But at the same time man is *deinon* because he is the violent one in the sense designated above. (He gathers the power and brings it to manifestness.) Man is the violent one, not aside from and along with other attributes but solely in the sense that in his fundamental violence [Gewalt-tätigkeit] he uses power [Gewalt] against the overpowering [Überwältigende]. Because he is twice *deinon* in a sense that is originally one, he is *to deinotaton,* the most powerful: violent in the midst of the overpowering.

But why do we translate *deinon* as "strange" [unheimlich]? Not in order to hide or attenuate the meaning of powerful, overpowering, violent; quite on the contrary. Because this *deinon* is meant as the supreme limit and link of man's being, the essence of the being thus defined should from the first be seen in its crucial aspect. But, in that case, is the designation of the powerful as the strange and uncanny [unheimlich] not a posterior notion derived from the impression that the powerful makes on us, whereas the essential here is to understand the *deinon* as what it intrinsically is? That is so, but we are not taking the strange in the sense of an impression on our states of feeling.

We are taking the strange, the uncanny [das Unheimliche], as that which casts us out of the "homely," i.e. the customary, familiar, secure. The unhomely [Unheimische] prevents us from making ourselves at home and therein it is overpowering. But man is the strangest of all, not only because he passes his life amid the strange understood in this sense but because he departs from his customary, familiar limits, because he is the violent one, who, tending toward the strange in the sense of the overpowering, surpasses the limit of the familiar [das Heimische].

To understand the full implication of these words of the chorus, we must bear this in mind: to say that man is *to deinotaton,* the strangest of all, is not to impute a particular attribute to man, as though he were also something else; no, the verse says that to be the strangest of all is the basic trait of the human essence, within which all other traits must find their place. In calling man "the strangest of all" it gives the authentic Greek definition of man. We shall fully appreciate this phenomenon of strangeness only if we experience the power of appearance and the struggle with it as an essential part of being-there.

The second passage that sustains the poetic edifice and rises above it is to be found in line 360, in the middle of the second strophe: *Pantoporos aporos ep'ouden erchetai.* "Everywhere journeying, inexperienced and without issue, he comes to nothingness." The essential words are *pantoporos aporos.* The word *poros* means: passage through . . . , transition to . . . , path. Everywhere man makes himself a path; he ventures into all realms of the essent, of the overpowering power, and in so doing he is flung out of all paths. Herein is disclosed the entire strangeness of this strangest of all creatures: not only that he tries the essent in the whole of its strangeness, not only that in so doing he *is* a violent one striving beyond his familiar sphere. No, beyond all this he becomes the strangest of all beings because, without issue on all paths, he is cast out of every relation to the familiar and befallen by *atē,* ruin, catastrophe.

It is not hard to see that this *pantoporos aporos* contains an interpretation of *deinotaton.*

The interpretation is completed in the third salient phrase, line 370: *hypsipolis apolis.* In construction it is similar to *pantoporos aporos,* and its situation in the middle of the antistrophe presents another parallel. But it moves in a different direction. It speaks not of *poros* but of *polis;* not of the paths to all the realms of the essent but of the foundation and scene of man's being-there, the point at which all these paths meet, the *polis. Polis* is usually translated as city or city-state. This does not capture the full meaning. *Polis* means, rather, the place, the there, wherein and as which historical being-there is. The *polis* is the historical place, the there *in* which, *out of* which, and *for* which history happens. To this place and scene of history belong the gods, the temples, the priests, the festivals, the games, the poets, the thinkers, the ruler, the council of elders, the assembly of the people, the army and the fleet. All this does not first belong to the *polis,* does not become political by entering into a relation with a statesman and a general and the business of the state. No, it is political, i.e. at the site of history, provided there be (for example) poets *alone,* but then really poets, priests *alone,* but then really priests, rulers *alone,* but then really rulers. *Be,* but this means: as violent men to use power, to become pre-eminent in historical being as creators, as men of action. Pre-eminent in the historical place, they become at the same time *apolis,* without city and place, lonely, strange, and alien, without issue amid the essent as a whole, at the same time without statute and limit, without structure and order, because they themselves *as* creators must first create all this.

The first phase shows us the inner design of the essence of the strangest of all beings, the realms and scope of his power and his destiny. Now we go back to the beginning and attempt the second phase of interpretation.

The second phase. In the light of what has been said above we now follow the sequence of the strophes and hear how the being of man, the strangest of beings, unfolds. We shall try to determine when the *deinon* is meant in the first sense, how the *deinon* in the second sense emerges concurrently, and how, in the reciprocal relation between the two, the being of the strangest being is built up before us in its essential form.

The first strophe names the sea and the earth, each of them overpowering (*deinon*) in its way. It does not speak of them in the manner of us moderns who experience them as mere geographical and geological phenomena and then, as though by an afterthought, brush them over with a few faint and fleeting emotions. Here "sea" is said as though for the first time; the poet speaks of the wintry waves that the sea creates as it unceasingly tears open its own depths and unceasingly flings itself into them. Immediately after the main, guiding statement of the first verses, the song begins, hard and powerful, with *touto kai polion*. Man embarks on the groundless deep, forsaking the solid land. He sets sail not upon bright, smooth waters but amid the storms of winter. The account of this departure concerts with the movement of the prosody; the word *chōrei* in line 336 is situated at the point where the meter shifts: *chōrei*, he abandons the place, he starts out—and ventures into the preponderant power of the placeless waves. The word stands like a pillar in the edifice of these verses.

But woven into one with this violent excursion [Aufbruch] upon the overpowering sea is the never-resting incursion [Einbruch] into the indestructible power of the earth. Here the earth is the highest of the gods. Violently, with acts of power [gewalt-tätig] man disturbs the tranquillity of growth, the nurturing and maturing of the goddess who lives without effort. Here the overpowering reigns not in self-consuming wildness but without effort and fatigue; from out of the superior tranquillity of great riches, it produces and bestows the inexhaustible treasure that surpasses all zeal. Into this power bursts the violent one; year after year he breaks it open with his plows and drives the effortless earth into his restless endeavor. Sea and earth, departure and upheaval are poined by the *kai* in line 334, to which corresponds the *te* in line 338.

And now to all this the antistrophe: it names the birds in the air, the denizens of the water, bull and stallion in the mountains. The living things, lightly dreaming, living in their own rhythm and their own precinct, perpetually overflowing into new forms yet remaining in their *one* channel, know the place where they wander and pass the night. As living things, they are embedded in the power of the sea and the earth. Into this life as it rolls along self-contained, extraordinary in its own sphere and structure and ground, man casts his snares and nets; he snatches the living creatures out of their order, shuts them up in his pens and enclosures, and forces them under his yokes. On the one hand eruption and upheaval. On the other capture and constraint.

At this point, before we pass to the second strophe and its antistrophe, it is necessary to insert a note calculated to ward off a misinterpretation of the whole poem—a misinterpretation to which modern man readily inclines and which is indeed frequent. We have already pointed out that this is no description and exposition of the activities and fields of activity of man, an essent among other essents, but a poetic outline of his being, drawn from its extreme possibilities and limits. This in itself precludes the interpretation of this chorus as a narrative of man's development from the savage hunter and primitive sailor to the civilized builder of cities. Such a notion is the product of ethnology and psychological anthropology. It stems from the unwarranted application of a natural science—and a false one at that—to man's being. The basic fallacy underlying such modes of thought consists in the belief that history begins with the primitive and backward, the weak and helpless. The opposite is true. The beginning is the strangest and mightiest. What comes afterward is not development but the flattening that results from mere spreading out; it is inability to retain the beginning; the beginning is emasculated and exaggerated into a caricature of greatness taken as purely numerical and quantitative size and extension. That strangest of all beings *is* what he is *because* he harbors such a beginning in which everything all at once burst from superabundance into the overpowering and strove to master it.

If this beginning is inexplicable, it is not because of any deficiency in our knowledge of history. On the contrary, the authenticity and greatness of historical knowledge reside in an understanding of the mysterious character of this beginning. The knowledge of primordial history is not a ferreting out of primitive lore or a collecting of bones. It is neither half nor whole natural science but, if it is anything at all, mythology.

The first strophe and antistrophe speak of the sea, the earth, the animal, as the overpowering power which bursts into manifestness through the acts of the violent one.

Outwardly the second strophe passes from a description of the sea, the earth, animals to a characterization of man. But no more than the first strophe and antistrophe speak of nature in the restricted sense does the second strophe speak only of man.

No, what is now named—language, understanding, sentiment, passion, building—are no less a part of the overpowering power than sea, earth, and animal. The difference is only that the latter, the power that is man's environment, sustains, drives, inflames him, while the former reigns within him as the power which he, as the essent that he himself is, must take upon himself.

This pervading force becomes no less overpowering because man takes it into his power, which he uses as such. All this merely conceals the uncanniness of language, of the passions, the powers by which man is ordained [gefügt] as a historical being, while it seems to him that it is *he* who disposes [verfügt] of them. The strangeness, the uncanniness of these powers resides in their seeming familiarity. Directly they yield themselves to man only in their nonessence [Unwesen], so driving him and holding him out of his essence. In this way he comes to regard what is fundamentally more remote and overpowering than sea and earth as closest of all to him.

How far man is from being at home in his own essence is revealed by his opinion of himself as he who invented and could have invented language and understanding, building and poetry.

How could man ever have invented the power which pervades him, which alone enables him to *be* a man? We shall be wholly forgetting that this song speaks of the powerful (*deinon*), the strange and uncanny, if we suppose that the poet makes man invent such things as building and language. The word *edidaxato* does not mean: man invented, but: he found his way to the overpowering and therein first found himself: the violent one, the wielder of power. In view of what has been said, the "himself" means at once he who breaks out and breaks up [ausbricht und umbricht, departs and plows], he who captures and subjugates.

It is this breaking out and breaking up, capturing and subjugating that opens up the essent *as* sea, *as* earth, *as* animal. It happens only insofar as the powers of language, of understanding, of temperament, and of building are themselves mastered [bewältigt] in violence. The violence of poetic speech, of thinking projection, of building configuration, of the action that creates states is not a function of faculties that man has, but a taming and ordering of powers by virtue of which the essent opens up as such when man moves into it. This disclosure of the essent is the power that man must master in order to become himself amid the essent, i.e. in order to be historical. What is meant by *deinon* here in the second strophe must not be misinterpreted as invention or as a mere faculty or attribute of man.

Only if we understand that the use of power in language, in understanding, in forming and building helps to create (i.e. always, to bring forth) the violent act [Gewalttat] of laying out paths into the environing power of the essent, only then shall we understand the strangeness, the uncanniness of all violence. For man, as he journeys everywhere, is not without issue in the external sense that he comes up against outward barriers and cannot go on. In one way or another he can always go farther into the etcetera. He is without issue because he is always thrown back on the paths that he himself has laid out: he becomes mired in his paths, caught in the beaten track, and thus caught he compasses the circle of his world, entangles himself in appearance, and so excludes himself from being. He turns round and round in his own circle. He can ward off whatever threatens this limited sphere. He can employ every skill in its place. The violence that originally creates the paths engenders its own mischief of versatility, which is intrinsically issueless, so much so that it bars itself from reflection about the appearance in which it moves.

All violence shatters against *one* thing. That is death. It is an end beyond all consummation [Vollendung], a limit beyond all limits. Here there is no breaking-out or breaking-up, no capture or subjugation. But this strange and alien [unheimlich] thing that banishes us once and for all from everything in which we are at home is no particular event that must be named among others because it, too, ultimately happens. It is not only when he comes to die, but always and essentially that man is without issue in the face of death. Insofar as man *is*, he stands in the issuelessness of death. Thus his being-there is the happening of strangeness. (For us this happening of a strangeness must be initially grounded in human being-there.)

With the naming of *this* strange and powerful thing, the poetic project of being and human essence sets its own limit upon itself.

For the second antistrophe does not go on to name *still* other powers but gathers those already named into their inner unity. The concluding strophe carries the whole back to its basic line. But as we have stressed in the first phase, the basic line of what is actually at the center of the song (the *deinotaton*) resides precisely in the unitary relation between the two meanings of *deinon*. Accordingly the final strophe, in summary, names three things.

1. The power, the powerful, in which the action of the violent one moves, is the entire scope of the machination (Machenschaft), *machanoen,* entrusted to him. We do not take the word "machina- tion" in a disparaging sense. We have in mind something essential that is disclosed to us in the Greek word *technē*. *Technē* means neither art nor skill, to say nothing of technique in the modern sense. We translate *technē* by "knowledge." But this requires expla- nation. Knowledge means here not the result of mere observations concerning previously unknown data. Such information, though indispensable for knowledge, is never more than accessory. Knowl- edge in the authentic sense of *technē* is the initial and persistent looking out beyond what is given at any time. In different ways, by different channels, and in different realms, this transcendence [Hinaussein] effects [setzt ins Werk] what first gives the datum its relative justification, its potential determinateness, and hence its limit. Knowledge is the ability to put into work the being of any particular essent. The Greeks called art in the true sense and the work of art *technē*, because art is what most immediately brings being (i.e. the appearing that stands there in itself) to stand, sta- bilizes it in something present (the work). The work of art is a work not primarily because it is wrought [gewirkt], made, but because it brings about [er-wirkt] being in an essent; it brings about the phenomenon in which the emerging power, *physis*, comes to shine [scheinen]. It is through the work of art as essent being that every- thing else that appears and is to be found is first confirmed and made accessible, explicable, and understandable as being or not being.

Because art in a pre-eminent sense stabilizes and manifests being in the work as an essent, it may be regarded as the ability, pure and simple, to accomplish, to put-into-the-work [ins-Werk-setzen], as *technē*. This accomplishment is a manifesting realization [Erwirken] of being *in* the essent. This superior, realizing opening and keeping open is knowledge. The passion of knowledge is inquiry. Art is knowledge and therefore *technē*. Art is not *technē* because it in- volves "technical" skill, tools, materials.

Thus *technē* provides the basic trait of *deinon*, the violent; for violence [Gewalt-tätigkeit] is the use of power [Gewalt-brauchen] against the overpowering [Überwältigende]: through knowledge it wrests being from concealment into the manifest as the essent.

2. Just as *deinon* as violence collects its essence in the fundamental Greek word *technē*, so *deinon* as the overpowering is manifested in the equally fundamental *dikē*. We translate it as Fug.[1] Here we understand Fug first in the sense of joint and framework [Fuge und Gefüge]; then as decree, dispensation, a directive that the overpowering imposes on its reign; finally, as the governing structure [das fügende Gefüge] which compels adaptation [Einfügung] and compliance [Sichfügen].

If *dikē* is translated as "justice" taken in a juridical, moral sense, the word loses its fundamental metaphysical meaning. The same applies to the interpretation of *dikē* as norm. In all its realms and dominions the overpowering, in respect to its domination, is Fug. Being, *physis*, as power, is basic and original togetherness: *logos;* it is governing order [fügender Fug]: *dikē.*

Thus the *deinon* as the overpowering (*dikē*) and the *deinon* as the violent (*technē*) confront one another, though not as two given things. In this confrontation *technē* bursts forth against *dikē*, which in turn, as Fug, the commanding order, disposes [verfügt] of all *technē*. The reciprocal confrontation *is.* It is only insofar as the strangest thing of all, being-human, is actualized, insofar as man is present as history.

3. The basic trait of the *deinotaton* lies in the interrelation between the two meanings of *deinon*. The sapient man sails into the very middle of the dominant order [Fug]; he tears it open and violently carries being into the essent; yet he can never master the overpowering. Hence he is tossed back and forth between structure and the structureless, order and mischief [Fug and Un-fug], between the evil and the noble. Every violent curbing of the powerful is either victory or defeat. Both, each in its different way, fling him out of home, and thus, each in its different way, unfold the dangerousness

---

[1] Heidegger is particularly free to define the word "Fug" as he wishes because the word does not occur in modern literary German except in the combination "mit Fug und Recht"—"with F. and justice," where it conveys no precise meaning but suggests "proper order," "fitness." This is why I have preferred to introduce the word in German. [TRANS.]

of achieved or lost being. Both, in different ways, are menaced by disaster. The *violent one,* the creative man, who sets forth into the un-said, who breaks into the un-thought, compels the unhappened to happen and makes the unseen appear—this violent one stands at all times in venture (*tolma,* line 371). In venturing to master being, he must risk the assault of the nonessent, *mē kalon,* he must risk dispersion, instability, disorder, mischief. The higher the summit of historical being-there, the deeper will be the abyss, the more abrupt the fall into the unhistorical, which merely thrashes around in issueless and placeless confusion.

Arrived at the end of the second phase, we may wonder what purpose can be served by a third.

The third phase. The central truth of the song was set forth in the first phase. The second phase has led us through all the essential realms of the powerful and violent. The final strophe pulls the whole together into the essence of him who is strangest of all. Certain details might be considered and elucidated more fully. But this would provide a mere appendage to what has already been said; it would not necessitate a new phase of interpretation. If we content ourselves with what the poem directly says, the interpretation is at an end. Actually it has just begun. The actual interpretation must show what does not stand in the words and is nevertheless said. To accomplish this the exegete must use violence. He must seek the essential where nothing more is to be found by the scientific interpretation that brands as unscientific everything that transcends its limits.

But here, where we must restrict ourselves to a single poem, we can undertake this third phase only from a limited point of view imposed by our main task, and even here we must confine ourselves to a few steps. Bearing in mind what has been said in the first phase, we start from the results of our explanation of the final strophe in the second phase.

The *deinotaton* of the *deinon,* the strangest of the strange, lies in the conflict between *dikē* and *technē.* The strangest is not the extreme rectilinear intensification of the strange. It is specifically the uniquely strange. The conflict between the overwhelming presence of the essent as a whole and man's violent being-there creates the possibility of downfall into the issueless and placeless: disaster. But disaster and the possibility of disaster do not occur only at the end, when a single act of power fails, when the violent one makes a false move; no, this disaster is fundamental, it governs and waits in the conflict between violence and the overpowering. Violence against the preponderant power of being *must* shatter against being, if being rules in its essence, as *physis,* as emerging power.

But this necessity of disaster can only subsist insofar as what must shatter is driven into such a being-there. Man is forced into such a being-there, hurled into the affliction [Not][2] of such being, because the overpowering as such, in order to appear in its power, *requires* a place, a scene of disclosure. The essence of being-human opens up to us only when understood through this need compelled by being itself. The being-there of historical man means: to be posited as the breach into which the preponderant power of being bursts in its appearing, in order that this breach itself should shatter against being.

The strangest (man) is what it is because, fundamentally, it cultivates and guards the familiar, only in order to break out of it and to let what overpowers it break in. Being itself hurls man into this breaking-away, which drives him beyond himself to venture forth toward being, to accomplish being, to stabilize it in the work, and so hold open the essent as a whole. Therefore the violent one knows no kindness and conciliation [Güte und Begütigung] (in the usual sense); he cannot be mollified or appeased by success or prestige. In all this the violent, creative man sees only the semblance of fulfillment, and this he despises. In willing the unprecedented, he casts aside all help. To him disaster is the deepest and broadest affirmation of the overpowering. In the shattering of the wrought work, in the knowledge that it is mischief [Unfug] and *sarma* (a dunghill), he leaves the overpowering to its order [Fug]. But all this not in the form of "psychic experiences" in which the soul of the creative man wallows, and still less in the form of petty feelings of inferiority, but wholly in terms of the accomplishment itself, the putting-

---

[2] The dictionary meanings of the German word "Not" are need, want, anguish, distress, affliction, peril, necessity. Insofar as one meaning can be disengaged from the whole, Heidegger's primary meaning is "need," because he has used this word "Not" as a translation for *chre* in the sixth fragment of Parmenides. But the word as used in German speech and poetry carries the primary implication of distress, trouble, affliction. [TRANS.]

into-the-work. *As history* the overpowering, being, is confirmed in works.

Thus the being-there of the historical man is the breach through which the being embodied in the essent can open. As such it is an *in-cident* [Zwischen-fall, a fall-between], the incident in which suddenly the unbound powers of being come forth and are accomplished as history. The Greeks had a profound sense of this suddenness and uniqueness of being-there, forced on them by being itself, which disclosed itself to them as *physis* and *logos* and *dikē*. It is inconceivable that the Greeks should have decided to turn out culture for the benefit of the next few millennia of Western history. In the unique need of their being-there they alone responded solely with violence, thus not doing away with the need but only augmenting it; and in this way they won for themselves the fundamental condition of true historical greatness.

We shall fail to understand the mysteriousness of the essence of being-human, thus experienced and poetically carried back to its ground, if we snatch at value judgments of any kind.

The evaluation of being-human as arrogance and presumption in the pejorative sense takes man out of his essential need as the in-cident. To judge in this way is to take man as something already-there, to put this something into an empty space, and appraise it according to some external table of values. But it is the same kind of misunderstanding to interpret the poet's words as a tacit rejection of being-human, a covert admonition to resign oneself without violence, to seek undisturbed comfort. This interpretation might even find some basis in the concluding lines of the poem.

One who is *thus* (namely the strangest of all) should be excluded from hearth and council. But the final words of the chorus do not contradict what has previously been said about being-human. Insofar as the chorus turns *against* the strangest of all, it says that this manner of being is *not* that of every day. Such being-there is not to be found in the usual bustle and activity. There is nothing surprising about these concluding words; indeed, we should have to be surprised if they were lacking. Their attitude of rejection is a direct and complete confirmation of the strangeness and uncanniness of human being. With its concluding words the song swings back to its beginning.

Oedipus Rex

by Sigmund Freud

In my experience, which is already extensive, the chief part in
the mental lives of all children who later become psycho-neurotics
is played by their parents. Being in love with one parent and hating
the other are among the essential constituents of the stock of psy-
chical impulses which is formed at that time and which is of such
importance in determining the symptoms of the later neurosis. It is
not my belief, however, that psycho-neurotics differ sharply in this
respect from other human beings who remain normal—that they
are able, that is, to create something absolutely new and peculiar
to themselves. It is far more probable—and this is confirmed by oc-
casional observations on normal children—that they are only distinguished by exhibiting on a magnified scale feelings of love and
hatred to their parents which occur less obviously and less intensely
in the minds of most children.

This discovery is confirmed by a legend that has come down
to us from classical antiquity: a legend whose profound and universal power to move can only be understood if the hypothesis I
have put forward in regard to the psychology of children has an
equally universal validity. What I have in mind is the legend of
King Oedipus and Sophocles' drama which bears his name.

Oedipus, son of Laius, King of Thebes, and of Jocasta, was exposed as an infant because an oracle had warned Laius that the
still unborn child would be his father's murderer. The child was
rescued, and grew up as a prince in an alien court, until, in doubts

as to his origin, he too questioned the oracle and was warned to avoid his home since he was destined to murder his father and take his mother in marriage. (On the road leading away from what he believed was his home, he met King Laius and slew him in a sudden quarrel. He came next to Thebes and solved the riddle set him by the Sphinx who barred his way. Out of gratitude the Thebans made him their king and gave him Jocasta's hand in marriage. He reigned long in peace and honour, and she who, unknown to him, was his mother bore him two sons and two daughters. Then at last a plague broke out and the Thebans made enquiry once more of the oracle. It is at this point that Sophocles' tragedy opens. The messengers bring back the reply that the plague will cease when the murderer of Laius has been driven from the land.

> But he, where is he? Where shall now be read
> The fading record of this ancient guilt?

The action of the play consists in nothing other than the process of revealing, with cunning delays and ever-mounting excitement—a process that can be likened to the work of a psychoanalysis—that Oedipus himself is the murderer of Laius, but further that he is the son of the murdered man and of Jocasta. Appalled at the abomination which he has unwittingly perpetrated, Oedipus blinds himself and forsakes his home. The oracle has been fulfilled.

Oedipus Rex is what is known as a tragedy of destiny. Its tragic effect is said to lie in the contrast between the supreme will of the gods and the vain attempts of mankind to escape the evil that threatens them. The lesson which, it is said, the deeply moved spectator should learn from the tragedy is submission to the divine will and realization of his own impotence. Modern dramatists have accordingly tried to achieve a similar tragic effect by weaving the same contrast into a plot invented by themselves. But the spectators have looked on unmoved while a curse or an oracle was fulfilled in spite of all the efforts of some innocent man: later tragedies of destiny have failed in their effect.

If *Oedipus Rex* moves a modern audience no less than it did the contemporary Greek one, the explanation can only be that its effect does not lie in the contrast between destiny and human will, but is to be looked for in the particular nature of the material on which that contrast is exemplified. There must be something which makes a voice within us ready to recognize the compelling force of destiny in the *Oedipus,* while we can dismiss as merely arbitrary such dispositions as are laid down in [Grillparzer's] *Die Ahnfrau* or other modern tragedies of destiny. And a factor of this kind is in fact involved in the story of King Oedipus. His destiny moves us only because it might have been ours—because the oracle laid the same curse upon us before our birth as upon him. It is the fate of all of us, perhaps, to direct our first sexual impulse towards our mother and our first hatred and our first murderous wish against our father. Our dreams convince us that that is so. King Oedipus, who slew his father Laius and married his mother Jocasta, merely shows us the fulfilment of our own childhood wishes. But, more fortunate than he, we have meanwhile succeeded, insofar as we have not become psychoneurotics, in detaching our sexual impulses from our mothers and in forgetting our jealousy of our fathers. Here is one in whom these primeval wishes of our childhood have been fulfilled, and we shrink back from him with the whole force of the repression by which those wishes have since that time been held down within us. While the poet, as he unravels the past, brings to light the guilt of Oedipus, he is at the same time compelling us to recognize our own inner minds, in which those same impulses, though suppressed, are still to be found. The contrast with which the closing Chorus leaves us confronted—

. . . Fix on Oedipus your eyes,
Who resolved the dark enigma, noblest champion and most wise.
Like a star his envied fortune mounted beaming far and wide:
Now he sinks in seas of anguish, whelmed beneath a raging tide . . .

—strikes as a warning at ourselves and our pride, at us who since our childhood have grown so wise and so mighty in our own eyes. Like Oedipus, we live in ignorance of these wishes, repugnant to morality, which have been forced upon us by Nature, and after their revelation we may all of us well seek to close our eyes to the scenes of our childhood.

There is an unmistakable indication in the text of Sophocles' tragedy itself that the legend of Oedipus sprang from some primeval dream-material which had as its content the distressing disturbance of a child's relation to his parents owing to the first stirrings of sexuality. At a point when Oedipus, though he is not yet enlightened, has begun to feel troubled by his recollection of the oracle, Jocasta consoles him by referring to a dream which many people dream, though, as she thinks, it has no meaning:

> Many a man ere now in dreams hath lain
> With her who bare him. He hath least annoy
> Who with such omens troubleth not his mind.

Today, just as then, many men dream of having sexual relations with their mothers, and speak of the fact with indignation and astonishment. It is clearly the key to the tragedy and the complement to the dream of the dreamer's father being dead. The story of Oedipus is the reaction of the imagination to these two typical dreams. And just as these dreams, when dreamt by adults, are accompanied by feelings of repulsion, so too the legend must include horror and self-punishment. Its further modification originates once again in a misconceived secondary revision of the material, which has sought to exploit it for theological purposes. (Cf. the dream-material in dreams of exhibiting.) The attempt to harmonize divine omnipotence with human responsibility must naturally fail in connection with this subject-matter just as with any other.

Sophocles' *Oedipus Tyrannus*

by Seth Benardete

Eine Sphinx, das ägyptische Gebilde des Rätsels selbst, sei in
Theben erschienen und habe ein Rätsel aufgegeben mit den
Worten: "Was ist das, was morgens auf vier Beinen geht, mit-
tags auf zweien und abends auf dreien?" Der Grieche Ödipus
habe das Rätsel gelöst und die Sphinx vom Felsen gestürzt,
indem er aussprach, dies sei der Mensch. Dies ist richtig; das
Rätsel der Ägypter ist der Geist, der Mensch, das Bewußtsein
seines eigentümlichen Wesens. Aber mit dieser alten Lösung
durch Ödipus, der sich so als Wissender zeigt, ist bei ihm die
ungeheuerste Unwissenheit gepaart über sich selbst und über
das, was er tut. Der Aufgang geistiger Klarheit in dem alten
Königshause ist noch mit Greueln aus Unwissenheit verbun-
den. Es ist die alte patriarchalische Herrschaft, der das Wissen
ein Heterogenes ist und die dadurch aufgelöst wird. Dies
Wissen wird erst gereinigt durch politische Gesetze; unmittel-
bar ist es unheilbringend. Das Selbstbewußtsein muß sich
noch, um zu wahrem Wissen und sittlicher Klarheit zu werden,
durch bürgerliche Gesetze und politische Freiheit gestalten
und zum schönen Geiste versöhnen.

G. W. F. Hegel, *Philosophie der Weltgeschichte*[1]

[1] It is said that a Sphinx, the Egyptian image for the riddle itself, appeared
in Thebes and proposed a riddle in these words: "What is it that goes on four
legs in the morning, two at noon, and three in the evening?" Oedipus the Greek
solved the riddle and toppled the Sphinx from its rock by declaring: It is Man.
This is correct; the riddle of the Egyptians is the Spirit, Man the Consciousness
of his own unique essence. But with this ancient solution through Oedipus, who
thus shows himself as a possessor of knowledge, he couples the most colossal
ignorance both about himself and about what he is doing. The emergence of
spiritual clarity in the ancient royal house is yet bound up with atrocities born

The crippled Oedipus, we must imagine, appears before the Thebans leaning on a staff, a staff which indicates as much his present authority as the use he once made of it to kill his father (811, cf. 456). The staff or scepter is thus triply significant: a support for his infirmity, a sign of his political position, and an instrument for patricide. In two of its uses the staff points to Oedipus' strength, in the other to his weakness; but this weakness no doubt enabled him to solve the riddle of the Sphinx: a man in the prime of life but maimed since childhood and hence "three-footed" before his time saw in himself the riddle's answer. He now, however, appears before a threefold division of his people, whose enigmatic character he fails to see:

> οἳ μὲν οὐδέπω μακρὰν
> πτέσθαι σθένοντες, οἳ δὲ σὺν γήρᾳ βαρεῖς
> ἱερῆς, ἐγὼ μὲν Ζηνός, οἳ δ᾽ ἔτ᾽ ἠθέων
> λεκτοί   (16-19)

> Some have not yet the strength to fly far; some are priests, heavy with old age, of whom I am the priest of Zeus; and some are selected from those still unmarried.

Children incapable of going far, priests weighed down with age, and a group of unmarried men stand before him. Oedipus is the only "man" (ἀνήρ), in the strict sense, who is present. Two of the groups are weak; the other is strong. Together they represent an anomalous and defective answer to the riddle of the Sphinx, for the aged appears as priests, and the two-footed man appears as bachelors. The suppliants for the city are either below or beyond generation: the children have not yet reached puberty, the youths have not yet become fathers, and the priests are presumably impotent. Only Oedipus has been and can be again a father. The absence of women, which in this way is underlined, points to the

---

of ignorance. It is the ancient patriarchal rule which became dissolved by the fact that its knowledge existed as a heterogeneity. This knowledge is only purified through political laws; in its unmediated form it is harmful. Self-consciousness, in order to attain to true knowledge and ethical clarity, still needs to be formed by civil laws and political freedom, and reconciled with the beautiful Spirit. G. W. F. Hegel, *Philosophy of History,* translated by Alexander Gelley.

blight that has now fallen on all generation. A bloody tempest, says the priest of Zeus, threatens to swamp the city:

φθίνουσα μὲν κάλυξιν ἐγκάρποις χθονός
φθίνουσα δ' ἀγέλαις βουνόμοις τόκοισί τε
ἀγόνοις γυναικῶν   (25-27, cf. 171-173, 270 ff.).

[The city] wastes away in the unopened fruitful buds of the earth; it wastes away in the herds of grazing cows and in the abortive births of women.

The fruit and the cattle perish, and the women abort in giving birth. Thebes has been struck by a plague that exactly fits Oedipus' crimes, for defective offspring is supposed to be the consequence of incest.[1] Oedipus, however, neither understands the meaning of the plague nor sees in the delegation anything defective. His first words— ὦ τέκνα ("O children")—suggest that he understands himself as father only in a metaphorical sense and is blind to the literal meaning of generation (cf. 1503-1506).[2] The play therefore moves from the question of who killed Laius to that of who generated Oedipus. It moves from a political to a family crime, which is, paradoxically, from the less comprehensive to the more comprehensive theme (cf. 635 ff.). Oedipus' discovery of his parents silently discloses his murder of Laius, but to discover himself as the murderer of Laius would not have disclosed his origins. Sophocles indicates this shift from one theme to the other by the absence of the word πόλις after its twenty-fifth occurrence at 880, the context of which is the denunciation of tyranny.[3] Tyranny links the political and the family crime.

The choral ode in which πόλις last occurs sees the tyrant as the transgressor of "laws that step on high, born in the heavenly aether, whose only father is Olympus, and which the mortal nature of men

---

[1] Xenophon *Memorabilia* IV. iv. 20-23.

[2] Perhaps, then, one should read at 1505, μή σφε, πάτερ, ἴδῃς ("Do not overlook them, father,") with J. Jackson, *Marginalia Scaenica* (London: Oxford Univ. Press, 1955), pp. 139 ff.

[3] ἀπόπτολις ("without a city") occurs at 1000 of Oedipus, ἄστυ ("city as buildings, walls, etc.") twice in the second half (1378, 1450). Jocasta addresses the chorus after the last mention of πόλις as χώρας ἄνακτες ("lords of the land") (911, cf. 631); Oedipus is called ἄναξ ("lord") fourteen times, only twice after 852, and both times by servants (1002, 1173).

did not give birth to" (865-870). These laws—there is no other mention of νόμος in the play—are the prohibitions against incest and patricide (cf. 823-833, 863 ff.). The tyrant's crimes are incest and patricide, for the tyrant is the paradigm of the illegal, and illegality seems best exemplified in the two crimes that stand closest to the unnatural both in the family and the city. As incest is paradigmatic for illegitimate birth, for no legal ceremony can render incestuous offspring legitimate, so patricide is paradigmatic for illegitimate succession, for it turns regicide into a crime that strikes at the heart of kingship (cf. 1, 58). Patricide, however, is only accidentally, whereas incest is necessarily, a political crime, for the city must be exogamous if the family is not to be self-sufficient and claim a loyalty greater than the city. The movement, therefore, from the question of who killed Laius to that of who generated Oedipus, while it goes deeper into the family, goes deeper into the city as well. Oedipus violates equally the public and the private with a single crime. He is the paradigm of the tyrant.

Oedipus is the completely public man. He has an openness and transparency that leave no room for the private and secret. When Creon asks him whether he should report what the oracle replied while the Chorus is present, Oedipus says, "Address it to all, for I bear a grief for these even more than for my soul" (93 ff.). The city in its public and private aspects alone counts, and Oedipus is a superfluous third:

> ἡ δ' ἐμὴ
> ψυχὴ πόλιν τε κἀμὲ καὶ σ' ὁμοῦ στένει   (63 ff.).

My soul sorrows together for the city, myself, and you [singular].

His own sorrow is neither the city's common nor each citizen's private sorrow; and it is in fact above and beyond either (cf. 1414 ff.), but Oedipus presents it as if it were only the union of the public and the private:

> εὖ γὰρ οἶδ' ὅτι
> νοσεῖτε πάντες, καὶ νοσοῦντες, ὡς ἐγὼ
> οὐκ ἔστιν ὑμῶν ὅστις ἐξ ἴσου νοσεῖ
> τὸ μὲν γὰρ ὑμῶν ἄλγος εἰς ἕν' ἔρχεται
> μόνον καθ' αὑτόν, κοὐδέν' ἄλλον   (59-63).

I know well that all of you are ill, and, though you are ill, there is no one of you who is as equally ill as I am, for your pain comes to one alone by himself and to no one else.

Everyone else is ill, but no one is as ill as Oedipus, for all the rest suffer individually, while he alone suffers collectively. He is a one like no other one. As ruler (ἄρχων) he is like the one that without being a number is the principle (ἀρχή) and measure of all numbers.[4] Oedipus' νόσος ("illness," "disease") is truly unequal to the citizens', for he is the source of theirs, but he regards himself as ill only because his grief is the sum of each partial grief. Oedipus always speaks for the city as a whole. Tiresias, for example, eight times refers to himself emphatically as ἐγώ, but never to the city, whereas Oedipus five times in the same scene refers to the city and only once to himself as ἐγώ: "But it was I, the know-nothing Oedipus, who came and stopped the Sphinx" (396 ff.). Oedipus immediately interprets Tiresias' reluctance to speak as a dishonor to the city and just cause for indignation (339 ff.). Tiresias' silence has nothing lawful (ἔννομα) in it, nor is it an act of kindness to the city that nurtured him (322 ff.). Oedipus' concern for his own deliverance seems to him to be nothing more than a rhetorical fullness of expression:

ῥῦσαι σεαυτὸν καὶ πόλιν, ῥῦσαι δ᾽ ἐμὲ
ῥῦσαι δε πᾶν μίασμα τοῦ τεθνηκότος   (312 ff., cf. 253 ff.).

Save yourself and the city, save me, and save [us] from the entire taint of the dead.

The third ῥῦσαι does not mean the same as the first two; but the deliverance from the pollution is in fact the same as the deliverance of the city from Oedipus. The city must be saved from Oedipus, whose own safety is incompatible with the safety of those with whom he allies himself (cf. 244 ff., 253 ff.). He appeals to the city as though he were the city and no one shared in it except himself (626-630, cf. 643). His utter publicity, his being only what he is as ruler of Thebes (cf. 443), makes him think the charges of Tiresias are prompted by private gain (380-389, cf. 124-126). He received the kingship as a gift, but had no desire for it, for he solved the riddle

---

[4] Aristotle *Metaphysica* 1016ᵇ 17-21; 1021ᵃ 12 ff.; *Physica* 220ᵃ 27.

of the Sphinx with complete disinterest (383 ff., 393 ff., cf. 540-542). As a stranger but lately enrolled in the city, he stands above all factional interests (219-222). His incorruptibility is the most evident sign that he lacks a private component; but the deepest sign is his crimes. The tyrant, says Socrates, commits those crimes (among which is incest) which most men only dream about (cf. 980-983). The dreams of others are the deeds of Oedipus. "For those awake," Heraclitus says, "there is a single and common order, but each one turns when asleep into his own" (fr. 89). Oedipus is always awake and a member of the common order (cf. 65). All the illegal desires of dreams, by being fulfilled in him, leave him empty of everything that is not public knowledge. He consists entirely of δόξα or seeming (cf. 1186-1196).

Seeming and likeness are opposed to what does not seem and resemble, but is. In the case of Oedipus, however, seeming and likeness always turn out to be true. He will seek the criminal, he says, as though he were fighting for the sake of his own father (264 ff.), because he holds the kingship Laius had before,

> ἔχων δὲ λέκτρα καὶ γυναῖχ᾽ ὁμόσπορον   (260).

Having the marriage bed and women of the same seedbed.

His wife is indeed ὁμόσπορος, not in the transferred sense that Laius and Oedipus share the same wife, but in the sense that Oedipus is literally kindred with her and sows the same seedbed where he himself was sown (cf. 460, 1210-1212). And what Oedipus then puts potentially—that if Laius had had children, they would be in common with his own—is now true of himself (261 ff., cf. 249-251). And finally, in calling Laius' murderer αὐτόχειρ (231, 266), he points to the murderer as one who killed in his own family.[5] The ordinary imprecision of speech always betrays Oedipus. Speech in his presence becomes literal and as univocal as mathematical definitions. Although "tyranny" and "tyrant" are loosely used throughout the play for "kingship" and "king," they prove in the end to be strictly true of Oedipus in his crimes.[6] If Creon uses the singular οἶκος

---

[5] Cf. Sophocles *Antigone* 172, 1175 ff.
[6] Βασιλεύς ("king") is only used twice in the play, once of Laius and once of Oedipus (257, 202), but τύραννος etc. ("tyrant") occurs fifteen times.

("house") three lines after Oedipus has used the plural, the change apparently has no significance (112, 115); but when Oedipus changes Creon's λῃσταί ("pirates," "robbers") into the singular, he has unwittingly pointed to the truth (122, 124, cf. 292 ff.). He asks Creon what prevented the Thebans from finding out who killed Laius (128 ff.). The Sphinx or "Constrictor" that asked about the four-footed, two-footed, and three-footed animal was in the way of their feet (ἐμποδών, cf. 445) and enticed them to look at what was at their feet (τὸ πρὸς ποσί) and neglect the obscure and invisible (τἀφανῆ, 130 ff.). Oedipus solved what was at their feet and he now is called upon to solve the invisible. He does not know that this distinction between the near and distant is no longer applicable. "I shall make it (αὖτ')," he says, "evident once more from the beginning"; and while he means τἀφανῆ, it is equally true of τὸ πρὸς ποσί, for his crippled feet finally identify him as the son of Laius and his murderer. The truth of Oedipus is right in front of him. There is nothing latent in him. He is the wholly unpoetic man, and hence it seems not accidental that in *Oedipus Tyrannus* alone of the seven plays we have of Sophocles the word μῦθος ("speech," "tale," "false tale") never occurs.[7]

The name of Oedipus perhaps most clearly shows that the surface truth of Oedipus is the truth of his depths as well. To be crippled was considered to be a sign of tyrannical ambitions (cf. 878), and the very name of the royal family, Labdacidae, contains within it λάβδα or lambda (λ), the letter which resembles an uneven gait.[8] Oedipus' name, then, as a sign of his defect, shows that the general truth expressed in the riddle of the Sphinx does not apply to himself. The answer "man" fails to cover the particular case of Oedipus. His defect, however, by placing him outside the species-characteristic of man, allowed him to see the species-characteristic. Oedipus has never reflected on his divergence from the species, nor understood why he alone could solve the riddle. The solution to the riddle depends on seeing that only one of the three kinds of feet literally holds. Oedipus saw the heterogeneity that underlies an artificial homogeneity, but he does not see his own disparity. Oedipus never

---

[7] In *Philoctetes* μῦθος does not occur before the appearance of Heracles (1410, 1417, 1447).

[8] Cf. Herodotus V. 92 β 1; Xenophon *Hellenica* III. iii. 3.

fits the groups in which he puts himself as a third element. The public, the private, and Oedipus do not make a genuine triad, any more than do the altars of Apollo, Athena, and Oedipus at which the Thebans sit (2, 16, 19-21, cf. 31), the alliance of Apollo, Laius, and Oedipus (244 ff.), or the joint rule of Jocasta, Creon, and Oedipus (577-581).⁹ The speciousness of the riddle's triad conceals a doubleness in man himself. He is a biped but an upright biped (cf. 419, 528, 1385), and his uprightness, which is shared by neither the baby nor the three-footed aged, indicates his ability to look up and know;¹⁰ and Oedipus, we learn, in spite of a lameness that would direct his glance downward to his feet, guided his flight from Corinth by looking at the stars (794-796).

Man is endowed with self-motion and awareness (cf. 6 ff., 396 ff.).¹¹ He is an οἶδε-πούς ("knows" "a foot") or Οἰδίπους, a pun the messenger from Corinth unknowingly makes when he asks the Chorus:

ἆρ' ἂν παρ' ὑμῶν, ὦ ξένοι, μάθοιμ' ὅπου
τὰ τοῦ τυράννου δώματ' ἐστὶν Οἰδίπου;
μάλιστα δ' αὐτὸν εἴπατ' εἰ κάτισθ' ὅπου   (924-926, cf. 43, 1128).¹²

Would I learn from you, strangers, where the palace of the tyrant Oedipus is? And, most of all, say if you know where he himself is.

Oedipus, who can see man in his motion, cannot see where (ποῦ) and on what basis he himself rests (cf. 367 ff., 413). The distant perspective his defect afforded him to see man in his three ages kept him from seeing the ground on which he himself stood. Oedipus' knowledge is divorced from his own body, but the crimes he committed are bodily crimes. His crimes have their origin in the privacy of the body (*his* mother and *his* father), and they are detected

⁹ The first triad is in Oedipus' first speech,

πόλις δ' ὁμοῦ μὲν θυμιαμάτων γέμει,
ὁμοῦ δέ παιάνων τε καὶ στεναγμάτων   (4 ff., cf. 64, 913–915).
The city is altogether full of incense, paeans, and groans.

Plutarch thrice quotes these lines as revealing of the soul, once likening them to Theophrastus' view of the triple source of music: enthusiasm, pleasure, and pain (*Quaestiones conviviales* I. 5 [623C–D]; cf. *de superstitione* 9 [169D]; *de virtute mor.* 6 [445D]; also Plato *Rep.* 573ᵃ 4 ff.).

¹⁰ Plato *Cratylus* 399ᶜ 1-6.

¹¹ Cf. Plato *Charmides* 159ᵇ 2-5.

¹² Cf. B. Knox, *Oedipus at Thebes* (New Haven: 1957), 183 ff.

through his body; but his own lack of privacy, which perfectly accords with the absence of all desires in Oedipus, leads him to look away from the body. He seems to stand at an Archimedean point. He somehow is pure mind.

Human knowledge, however, unlike divine or divinely inspired knowledge, does not have the purity and openness that Oedipus thinks it has. The Chorus suggests to Oedipus that Apollo should properly disclose who killed Laius, but Oedipus reminds them that no one can compel the gods against their will (278-281). The Chorus has another suggestion, and Oedipus allows them even a third (282 ff.). Tiresias is the second possibility, and though Tiresias is provoked by anger into speaking, the truth that he tells is completely useless. Tiresias does not offer, perhaps because he cannot, any evidence for what he says. He is as enigmatic and teasing as was the drunken Corinthian who started Oedipus on his quest for his origins (779-786). The one clue there is (cf. 118-121)—this is the third suggestion of the Chorus—is the "dumb and ancient tale" that some wayfarers slew Laius (290). The single clue is false, but it is still a clue. Human error, like the defective feet of Oedipus, leads to the truth, while divine knowledge is either unavailable or enigmatic.[13] The lone survivor of Laius' retinue had out of fear exaggerated the number of attackers (cf. 119 ff.); but if he had not, "one could never prove equal to many" (845, cf. 120), and Oedipus would not be the murderer. The clue is a false arithmetic. Jocasta is certain that there were many, for the city heard it, and not she alone (848-850). What is publicly made manifest cannot be untrue. Both Jocasta and Oedipus identify the evident with the city, but the city lies wrapped in opinion which only parades as knowledge. And yet Oedipus can test this falsehood, while he finds the truth, which is naturally inborn in Tiresias (299), refractory to testing (cf. 498-511). Tiresias' blindness prevents him from ever knowing where

---

[13] The tribrach φονέα ("murderer") occurs three times as the first foot in the line (362, 703, 721), twice of Oedipus as the murderer of Laius, and the third time in Jocasta's denial that Laius' son killed him; but what Jocasta says starts a ψυχῆς πλάνημα κἀνακίνησις φρενῶν ("a wandering of the soul and agitation of the wits") in Oedipus (727), which is also the third and last time that Oedipus refers to his soul (64, 94). And again πότερον(α) ("whether") occurs three times at the beginning of the line (112, 750, 960), twice of Laius, once of Polybus, Oedipus' supposed father.

he is, but the sacredness that keeps him detached from human and political things allows him to be unconcerned with the ground of his knowledge. Oedipus mockingly asks Tiresias why he did not solve the riddle of the Sphinx (390-394). The answer is plain: the riddle has a wholly human answer, and Tiresias knows about man only in his relation to the gods. Oedipus, unsupported by any extra-human knowledge—"the know-nothing Oedipus" (397)—solves it because he is himself the paradigm of man (1193-1196). Oedipus represents the human attempt to replace the sacred—his failure to return to Corinth is his denial of oracles—[14] by the purely human. He is to be the third element alongside the public and the private (cf. 16, 31-34). The purely human, however, seems to entail not only the destruction of the sacred, but the collapse of any distinction between the public and the private. The purely human, at least as Oedipus reveals it, will prove to be the monstrous.

The Chorus is outraged that anyone should disbelieve the oracles (883-910). The oracles are three in number. One foretold that Laius would be killed by his own son, another that Oedipus would kill his father and marry his mother, and the third said that the presence in Thebes of Laius' murderer caused the plague. The Chorus wants all three oracles to turn out to be true, but it also wants its own lot ($\mu o \hat{\iota} \rho \alpha$) to be such that the Chorus does not break the sacred prohibitions against patricide and incest (862-872). Oedipus, on the other hand, wants the oracle addressed to himself to prove false, so that human morality will be maintained; but the gods want the authority of all the oracles, i.e., their own authority, maintained even at the expense of human morality. Human morality, however, was not brought about by human nature: Olympus alone was its father. It is the nature of Oedipus, then, to break these laws, but he does not know that it is his nature. He believes it to be the work of Apollo (1329 ff., cf. 376 ff.). Oedipus, who thinks himself the manifestation of the city, turns out to be the manifestation of human nature itself, and the fate of human nature by itself is to violate the divine laws of the city. *Hybris* is the natural in man, and man is naturally a tyrant (873). *Hybris* makes man rise to heights he can-

---

[14] 794-797, cf. 855-859, 897-910, 964-972.

not maintain and hence plunges him into sheer compulsion, "where he wields a useless foot" (873-879). The swollen foot that is Oedipus finally trips him up.

Even if Oedipus lacks any secret desires, he still is not free from all passions. His overriding passion is anger. He first shows it when Tiresias refuses to speak. "You would enrage," he tells him, "the nature of a stone," so unmoved does he think Tiresias (334-336). "You blame my temper," Tiresias replies, "but do not see your own that dwells with you." Tiresias' ὀργή ("temper," "anger") is his indifference to the city, Oedipus' ὀργή, which is all of Oedipus, is his concern for the city. "Who would not become enraged on hearing such words as yours," he answers Tiresias, "in which you dishonor the city?" Oedipus' anger is entirely at the service of the city. His anger now expresses his private devotion to public justice, though the same anger once brought him to kill Laius and his retinue (807). Oedipus cannot stand opposition. He must overcome everything that resists him (cf. 1522 ff.). He fails to see any difference between his indignation at an injury to himself and one to the city (629, 642 ff.). His indignation is a passion for homogeneity (cf. 408 ff.). Everything must be reduced to the same level or eliminated until he alone as the city remains.[15] The sacred in the person of Tiresias and the private in that of Creon must go (cf. 577-582). He is opposed to the Chorus' wish that god never dissolve noble contention and rivalry in the city (879-881). His belief that he is a unique one in the city is rooted in his total public-spiritedness, but the passion he brings to that role also looks toward his crimes against the city. Anger as the leveller of distinctions resembles the homogeneity of law—there can be no exceptions to Oedipus' decree, not even himself (816-820)—but this extreme reductionism in Oedipus' anger duplicates another kind of homogeneity that comes from his crimes.

νῦν δ' ἄθεος μέν εἰμ', ἀνοσίων δὲ παῖς,
ὁμογενὴς δ' ἀφ' ὧν αὐτὸς ἔφυν τάλας   (1360 ff.)

Now I am without god and the son of unholy [parents], but I alas am of the same kind as those from whom I was born.

[15] Cf. Herodotus V. 92 ζ-η 1.

Oedipus is of the same kind as those from whom he was born. He is equally husband and son of Jocasta, father and brother of Antigone, and killer of Laius who gave him life (457-460, cf. 1403-1407). By killing his father and marrying his mother, he has destroyed the triad of father, mother, and son. He is not a third one over and beyond his origins, but he is at one with them (cf. 425). He is in his being the reduction that he tries to carry out with his anger. The law against incest that forbids homogeneity in the family emerges in his violation of it as the homogeneity of anger. Oedipus' anger is the surface expression of his incest. They share in common the exclusive care and defense of his own without concern for anything alien; and this exclusiveness is characteristic of the city which Oedipus has made his own. His public anger and his private incest therefore come together in the Thebans' belief in their autochthony. Autochthony would give the earth to everyone as a common mother and hence make incest inevitable; but it would also best justify a city's exclusive possession of its land and hence most inspire the citizens to defend it.[16] The Chorus divines that Oedipus will share with Cithaeron a common fatherland—it will be his πατριώτης —and that Cithaeron will prove to be his nurse and mother as well (1086-1092). Oedipus, however, turns out to be autochthonous in another nonmetaphorical sense.

$$\pi\tilde{\omega}\varsigma\ \pi o\tau\epsilon\ \pi\tilde{\omega}\varsigma\ \pi o\theta'\ \alpha\acute{\iota}\ \pi\alpha\tau\rho\tilde{\omega}—$$
$$\alpha\acute{\iota}\ \sigma'\ \ddot{\alpha}\lambda o\kappa\epsilon\varsigma\ \phi\acute{\epsilon}\rho\epsilon\iota\nu,\ \tau\acute{\alpha}\lambda\alpha\varsigma,$$
$$\sigma\hat{\iota}\gamma'\ \dot{\epsilon}\delta\upsilon\nu\acute{\alpha}\theta\eta\sigma\alpha\nu\ \dot{\epsilon}\varsigma\ \tau o\sigma\acute{o}\nu\delta\epsilon;\qquad (1210\text{-}1212).$$

How, how could the father's furrows, alas, bear to keep silence for so long?

His father's furrows are Jocasta's loins and not Theban territory (cf. 1482-1485, 1497 ff., 1502). What would have been the complete vindication of Oedipus as the city if the πατρῷαι ἄλοκες had been the πατρῷα λαῖα ("earth" or "land"), signifies instead his greatest crime against the city.[17] Oedipus, then, in destroying the ground of the private, reveals the ground of the public. In his violation of the unwritten law he is the truth of civil law. But Oedipus

---

[16] Cf. Plato *Rep.* 414^d1-^e6.
[17] Cf. Herodotus VI. 107. 1-2.

is also the nature of man as it appears in itself without the restraint of divine law. Thus the monstrousness of Oedipus consists in his being together the ultimately natural (the private) and the ultimately lawful (the public) in man.

Oedipus believes that Jocasta, ashamed of his base birth, does not want the herdsman to be questioned; but he insists on discovering his origins even if they are small. "I count myself the son of beneficent chance," he says. "She is my natural mother, and the months that are my congeners made me small and great" (1080-1083, cf. 1090). Oedipus is the son of chance and the sport of time. Jocasta had asked him, "Why should a human being be afraid, for whom the ways of chance are sovereign, and there is clear foreknowing of nothing? It is best to live at random" (977-979). If chance controls Oedipus because he is its offspring, he has nothing to fear from any disclosures that time might bring (1213-1215, cf. 917). They would all be as indifferent to him as they are to chance. The lack of discrimination in chance—that is, its randomness— necessarily leads to the loss in Oedipus of any distinctions, and that is his crime. Chance is the ground of his apparent unconditionality, for his crimes have uprooted his own origins and made him his own ἀρχή ("origin," "principle"). He is completely free. The one condition attached to his freedom is his swollen feet, but they are literally Oedipus himself. He stands in the way of his own nature (cf. 674 ff.). Oedipus says that he met Laius at a triple road, but Jocasta calls the meeting of the ways from Daulia and Delphi a split road (733, 800 ff., cf. 1399). A τριπλὴ ὁδός ("triple way") is the same as a σχιστὴ ὁδός ("split way"). Two is the same as three. If one is walking a road and comes to a branching of it, there are only two ways that one can go, for the third way has already been traversed. If, however, one is not walking but simply looking at a map of such a branching, there appear to be three ways to take. Action sees only two where contemplation sees three. Oedipus places himself in the camp of θεωρία, but it is a naive θεωρία. He thinks he has one more degree of freedom than he has. If his swollen feet are the sign of this double perspective, his crimes, one might say, are its truth. He has, in committing incest, made literal the metaphor of political theory. Even as dreaming and waking are for him one and the same (cf. 980-983), so he is blind to the difference between theory and practice. The distant and the near view are in him merged: τάφανές ("the invisible") is τὸ πρὸς ποσίν ("that which is at the feet").

Oedipus wants to become invisible to mortals before the double guilt of incest and patricide overtakes him (830-833). And he later effects his invisibility by blinding himself, for he lives so entirely in the realm of δόξα, of seeming, opinion, and reputation—the famous Oedipus is the know-nothing Oedipus (7, 397)—that his inability to see is equivalent to his not being seen (cf. 1371-1374). "This day," Tiresias had told him, "shall bring you to birth and destroy you" (438). The day that brings Oedipus into the light takes away his light (cf. 375, 1375 ff.). His blindness has made him who was completely transparent opaque. He is now σκοτεινός (1326). In thus turning away from the sham clarity of δόξα into himself (1317 ff., 1347 ff.), Oedipus restores the private that he had destroyed. He recovers his shame. "If you no longer feel ashamed before the generations of mortals," Creon tells him, "at least feel shame before the all-nourishing light of the sun, to show unhidden such a taint that not earth, not sacred rain, not light will welcome. Go into the house at once: it is holy only for those who are kin to see and hear kindred evils" (1424-1431).[18] Not just the city, but the world itself turns its back on Oedipus. He had forbidden any citizen from receiving or addressing the murderer of Laius, from sharing with him the prayers or sacrifices to the gods, and from granting him the use of lustral waters (238-240); but now the crime of incest has withdrawn Oedipus from things that are beyond the civil order. He must return to the private. And yet Oedipus does not need the seclusion of a house in order to retire from the world; his blinding of himself has already done it for him. His own concern is for his banishment from the city, whose physical presence (ἄστυ), whose towers, whose sacred statues of the gods he no longer dares to look upon (1377 ff). The restoration of the private must be accompanied by the restoration of the public which he had equally destroyed. He therefore is at the end what he was at the beginning, a superfluous third.

As the report (φήμη or φάτις) of oracles has been confirmed in the light (φῶς) of truth (151-158, 1440) (the two words share linguistically

---

[18] Cf. Euripides *Phoenissae* 63-66; frs. 553, 683.

the same root [cf. 472-476]),[19] so the unseeable Oedipus is also the unspeakable Oedipus:

> ἰὼ σκότου
> νέφος ἐμὸν ἀπότροπον, ἐπιπλόμενον ἄφατον   (1313 ff.).
>
> O, my abominable cloud of darkness hovering, unspeakable.

He is surrounded by silence and darkness (1337-1339). If there had been some way to stop his ears, he says, he would not have held back from closing off his body (1386-1389). He would no longer hear, as he longer sees, his crimes. He would deprive himself of sense, as he was once deprived of motion.[20] He would cut off the knowing as he was cut off from the walking in his name. He had abused Tiresias as blind in his ears, his mind, and his eyes (371); but he himself now wants to hear and see rothing:

> τὸ γὰρ
> τὴν φροντίδ' ἔξω τῶν κακῶν οἰκεῖν γλ ιcύ   (1389 ff.).
>
> For thought to dwell outside of evils is sweet.

Oedipus forgets to put out his mind. He does not regard νοῦς as a third faculty distinct from hearing and sight. He is like Plato's Theaetetus, whose mathematical knowledge rests on his thinking, but who believes that knowledge is sensation. The Chorus calls Oedipus equally wretched for his calamities as for his reflection (νοῦς) on them (1347), and Oedipus himself, when he cannot see, reflects on the wretched future of his daughters (1486 ff.). In spite of his own practice, he does not consider that thinking is irreducible to sense, just as he did not understand that his ability to solve the riddle of the Sphinx revealed more about man than did his answer. Man is the being that solves riddles. The difference between man as two-footed and man as three- or four-footed does not consist in his being literally a biped—the δίπους in Oedipus' name—and only metaphorically three- and four-footed, but in his thinking. The homogeneity which Oedipus discovered in his origins has made him

---

[19] *Anecdota Graeca,* ed. J. A. Cramer (Oxford: At the University Press, 1839-1841), Vol. I, pp. 428, 19-23.

[20] ἄρθρα, which literally means "joints," occurs three times, twice of Oedipus' pinned ankles, and once of his eyes that he blinded with Jocasta's pins (718, 1032, 1270).

blind to this heterogeneous element. Oedipus discovered the speciousness of the triad in the riddle, but he then found that the heterogeneity of mother, father, and son concealed in his case a sameness. He distinguished a difference in what the riddle had presented as a sameness, only to discover a sameness beneath an apparent difference. His thinking as differentiating found itself confronted with the undifferentiable. The single night in which his blindness has cast him seems to be truer than the daylight of his understanding (cf. 374 ff.). His anger in finally turning on himself condemns him to live the homogeneity of his crimes.

The first indication that Laius might be Oedipus' father occurs when Oedipus asks Jocasta what the nature (φύσις) of Laius was, and she says that he did not differ much from the shape (μορφή) of Oedipus (740-743). They look alike because Oedipus is the son of Laius, but Oedipus, in killing his father and marrying his mother, points to a deeper sameness in generation itself. He is not different from his origins. He is the same as that from which he came. He is the son of chance. Not the *eidos* of man, which the Sphinx had posed as a riddle, but his *genesis* is the riddle of man. An artificial riddle yields to a natural riddle, and Oedipus is thrice characterized by his nature. He says himself that Tiresias' silence would anger the nature even of a stone (334 ff.), and the nature of stone is to be without sex and human shape;[21] while Creon says that Oedipus' nature is his θυμός ("spirit," "anger," "heart"), which makes itself almost too painful to be borne (674 ff., cf. 914, 975); and Jocasta says that Oedipus' nature or shape was close to Laius'. Oedipus has a threefold nature: his potential shapelessness, his θυμός, his generated shape. His θυμός is unbearable because it shows through his crimes that his generated shape only hides his potential shapelessness. Oedipus' crimes seem to have uncovered the undifferentiated beginnings of man. They point to his nonanthropomorphic ἀρχαί. As violations of divine law they point to the ἀρχαί that lie behind the anthropomorphic gods. If the Olympian gods gave man their own shape (cf. 1097-1109), the prohibitions against incest and patricide would mean that man was not to search into the shapeless elements beyond these gods. If he did he would find Chaos with its

---

[21] Cf. *Odyssey* XIX. 163.

offspring Night and all things mixed together. He would find Uranus as the son and husband of Earth—the prime example of incest in the Greek theogony—and Uranus castrated by his own son.[22] Oedipus, then, who discovered what man is in his *eidos*, seems to have discovered in his *hybris* the nonhuman *genesis* of man. The whole of earth, sacred rain, and light, of which Creon forbids Oedipus to be a part, must be informed by the sacred if it justly is to exclude Oedipus (1424-1428, cf. 238-240, 1378 ff.). The sacred must bind together and keep apart the public (light) and the private (earth).[23] If the whole does not have this bond of Olympian sacredness, which guarantees the human in man, then Oedipus, whose θυμός points jointly to the homogeneity of law and the homogeneity of nature, is truly the inhuman paradigm of man. This is the question which the three particles that most nearly make up the name of Oedipus, οὐ δή που ("Surely not?"), can be said to introduce—a question raised in utter disbelief, but sometimes answered affirmatively (cf. 1042, 1472).[24]

In *Oedipus at Colonus*, we learn that Oedipus, toward the end of his life, came to the bronze-stepped threshold rooted in the earth (1590 ff.), where Hesiod says grow the roots, the beginnings, and the ends of earth, sea, and sky;[25] and that just after his disappearance Theseus was seen reverencing together in a single speech Earth and the Olympus of the gods (1653-1655).

[22] Hesiod *Theogony* 116-136, 176-181.
[23] Cf. Sophocles *Antigone* 1066-1073.
[24] Cf. Sophocles *Antigone* 380 ff.
[25] *Theogony* 726-728, 736-741, 811-813.

On Sophocles' *Electra*

by *Virginia Woolf*

Sophocles would take the old story of Electra, for instance, but would at once impose his stamp upon it. Of that, in spite of our weakness and distortion, what remains visible to us? That his genius was of the extreme kind in the first place; that he chose a design which, if it failed, would show its failure in gashes and ruin, not in the gentle blurring of some insignificant detail; which, if it succeeded, would cut each stroke to the bone, would stamp each finger-print in marble. His Electra stands before us like a figure so tightly bound that she can only move an inch this way, an inch that. But each movement must tell to the utmost, or, bound as she is, denied the relief of all hints, repetitions, suggestions, she will be nothing but a dummy, tightly bound. Her words in crisis are, as a matter of fact, bare; mere cries of despair, joy, hate

οὖ 'γὼ τάλαιν', ὅλωλα τῇδ' ἐν ἡμέρᾳ.
παῖσον, εὖ σθένεις, διπλῆν.

But these cries give angle and outline to the play. It is thus, with a thousand differences of degree, that in English literature Jane Austen shapes a novel. There comes a moment—"I will dance with you," says Emma—which rises higher than the rest, which, though not eloquent in itself, or violent, or made striking by beauty of language, has the whole weight of the book behind it. In Jane Austen, too, we have the same sense, though the ligatures are much less tight, that her figures are bound, and restricted to a few

definite movements. She, too, in her modest, everyday prose, chose
the dangerous art where one slip means death.

But it is not so easy to decide what it is that gives these cries of
Electra in her anguish their power to cut and wound and excite.
It is partly that we know her, that we have picked up from little
turns and twists of the dialogue hints of her character, of her appearance, which, characteristically, she neglected; of something
suffering in her, outraged and stimulated to its utmost stretch of
capacity, yet, as she herself knows ("my behaviour is unseemly and
becomes me ill"), blunted and debased by the horror of her
position, an unwed girl made to witness her mother's vileness and
denounce it in loud, almost vulgar, clamour to the world at large.
It is partly, too, that we know in the same way that Clytemnestra
is no unmitigated villainess. "θεινὸν τὸ τίκτειν ἐστίν," she says—"there
is a strange power in motherhood". It is no murderess, violent and
unredeemed, whom Orestes kills within the house, and Electra bids
him utterly destroy—"strike again". No; the men and women
standing out in the sunlight before the audience on the hillside
were alive enough, subtle enough, not mere figures, or plaster
casts of human beings.

Yet it is not because we can analyse them into feelings that they
impress us. In six pages of Proust we can find more complicated
and varied emotions than in the whole of the *Electra*. But in the
Electra or in the *Antigone* we are impressed by something different,
by something perhaps more impressive—by heroism itself, by fidelity
itself. In spite of the labour and the difficulty it is this that draws
us back and back to the Greeks; the stable, the permanent, the
original human being is to be found there. Violent emotions are
needed to rouse him into action, but when thus stirred by death,
by betrayal, by some other primitive calamity, Antigone and Ajax
and Electra behave in the way in which we should behave thus
struck down; the way in which everybody has always behaved; and
thus we understand them more easily and more directly than we
understand the characters in the *Canterbury Tales*. These are the
originals, Chaucer's the varieties of the human species.

It is true, of course, that these types of the original man or
woman, these heroic Kings, these faithful daughters, these tragic
Queens who stalk through the ages always planting their feet in

the same places, twitching their robes with the same gestures, from habit not from impulse, are among the greatest bores and the most demoralising companions in the world. The plays of Addison, Voltaire, and a host of others are there to prove it. But encounter them in Greek. Even in Sophocles, whose reputation for restraint and mastery has filtered down to us from the scholars, they are decided, ruthless, direct. A fragment of their speech broken off would, we feel, colour oceans and oceans of the respectable drama. Here we meet them before their emotions have been worn into uniformity. Here we listen to the nightingale whose song echoes through English literature singing in her own Greek tongue. For the first time Orpheus with his lute makes men and beasts follow him. Their voices ring out clear and sharp; we see the hairy tawny bodies at play in the sunlight among the olive trees, not posed gracefully on granite plinths in the pale corridors of the British Museum. And then suddenly, in the midst of all this sharpness and compression, Electra, as if she swept her veil over her face and forbade us to think of her any more, speaks of that very nightingale: "that bird distraught with grief, the messenger of Zeus. Ah, queen of sorrow, Niobe, thee I deem divine—thee; who evermore weepest in thy rocky tomb".

And as she silences her own complaint, she perplexes us again with the insoluble question of poetry and its nature, and why, as she speaks thus, her words put on the assurance of immortality. For they are Greek; we cannot tell how they sounded; they ignore the obvious sources of excitement; they owe nothing of their effect to any extravagance of expression, and certainly they throw no light upon the speaker's character or the writer's. But they remain, something that has been stated and must eternally endure.

The Electra of Sophocles

by Thomas Woodard

The *Electra* turns around Electra, but in order to appreciate her we must appreciate her play. Therefore let us take the *Electra* as a whole for our point of departure. What place does Electra occupy in it? What is her role in the history and action that absorbs us from beginning to end?

We may approach an answer by realizing that Electra is curiously alienated from one level of action through most of the drama. For at the outset Orestes and his men set in motion a plot to overthrow Clytemnestra and Aegisthus which continues, unabated, more or less behind the scenes, until it reaches complete fruition; reminders of it occur indirectly in every episode, and quite overtly when the Paedagogus enters to tell his false tale. The myth of the *Electra,* indeed, virtually passes over the heroine; as Aeschylus did in his *Oresteia.* History is made, in other words, even when Electra is oblivious of it. She initiates little of this larger action, and participates in it enthusiastically only after rebuke, and only in the closing minutes. And we must admit that this myth of vengeance could have provided a thrilling play by itself, without the presence of Electra; that in fact it does create suspense throughout the play as it stands, and dominates the finale. Electra's predicament is resolved, if at all, only in the resolution of the history of Orestes' return and revenge.

The structure of the *Electra* makes the heroine stand on stage

"The Electra of Sophocles" by Thomas Woodard. Portions of this essay have appeared in "*Electra* by Sophocles: the Dialectical Design," *Harvard Studies in Classical Philology,* LXVIII (1964). Copyright © 1964 by the President and Fellows of Harvard College. Reprinted by permission of the Harvard University Press.

in the midst of an initially alien world, that of the men's plot, and play out her drama in relation to this, merging with it toward the end. More exactly, she lives out her own history while the men are making history in another sense; the *Electra* develops two kinds of action simultaneously, one in counterpoint with the other. We may describe these two kinds of action, these two dramatic *genres*, in terms of the theater of the fifth century B.C. The men act in high melodrama, serious, suspenseful, noble, and successful; Electra lives in the *agones,* or conflicts and suffering, of the older tragedy.

If this duality informs the *Electra,* Electra's experience cannot be simple. She must find her place in a larger order, the play as a whole; she must come into relation with a contrasting order, the world of the men. And so she does, superbly. Unlike Aeschylus, Sophocles makes Electra the focal point; and she overpowers the men's plot with her own strength and passion. We almost cease to feel suspense about revenge in our concern for her. Her figure dwarfs all others. In short, her tragedy bursts out of the framework of the double plot, just as her form of heroic action seems incommensurable with the men's activities.

For Electra dominates the *Electra* excessively: her speaking part is one of the longest in Greek tragedy; she remains in full view nine-tenths of the time; she includes the heights and depths of emotion in her range; she chants more lyrics than any other Sophoclean protagonist. We must suspect that these excesses of speech, stamina, passion, and lyric express something essential to Sophocles' conception of his heroine. At the same time, we are struck by what would ordinarily be outright defects: her ignorance of Orestes' return and strategy; her physical inactivity; her wrangling and iteration; her mistaken opinons; her hate. Yet these too seem to contribute to her power in the theater; these too must be essential to her heroic character.

We begin to appreciate Electra's world when we realize how in all her traits she defines herself by antithesis to the men. They are laconic; move on and off the stage with facility; display little feeling; have no lyrics. They know what's afoot; and behave with restraint, prudence, reasonableness. In fact, the men's dramatic personalities oppose Electra's at every point. As in action and *genre,* the *Electra* combines two distinct kinds of character.

In the course of her history Electra changes. At the beginning she is poles apart from the men. But by the time Orestes rejoins her, she has developed toward him in certain respects, so that they can work as partners in the finale. The present interpretation sees a dialectical pattern in the initial separation and subsequent reunion of brother and sister, and sees dialectic throughout in Electra's struggles and debates, internal and external. But when all is said and done, Electra triumphs. Though paired with Orestes, she is incomparable; and all the antitheses in the play are similarly imbalanced.

The Prologue scene initiates the design of dialectic and imbalanced antithesis. It has one feature unique in the extant work of Sophocles: it is divided between characters who neither address one another nor occupy the stage together. The separation of brother and sister, and the astonishing differences between the feelings and thoughts expressed by each, present to our eyes and minds a number of fundamental contrasts, built into the divided scene. And while the men's half of the Prologue prepares for the entrance of Electra, the intensity of our response to her presupposes a response to them, since she startles us out of a world that we have taken for granted. We enter Electra's world, then, through a door provided by the play, the men's world.

In the theater what we see and hear coalesce, or rather exist as one. The contrasts in the Prologue are all self-evident in the sense that they are present in what the characters do, say, evoke, and imply. The halving of the Prologue corresponds to a number of dualities, but most obvious, perhaps, is that of the sexes. First three men occupy the stage, then Electra, who is soon joined by the chorus of women. Sophocles found this dramatic contrast close at hand, in the rigorous social differentiation of men and women in fifth-century Athens. Women tended the home while able-bodied men controlled all public affairs as well as trades.

We see the Paedagogus and Orestes confidently, rationally, briskly planning a course of action. And both conclude their opening speeches with references to *erga,* acts, deeds, exhorting one another to set to work. *Ergon* implies not only many specifically male livelihoods and their products, but "job" or "industry," "possessions" in general, and "interest" in the economic sense. So also both men stress the *kairos,* which means "profit" as well as "the right time." Their avowed goal in fact is *kerdos,* gain, profit, and wealth; they are even willing to get it by theft if necessary. Orestes announces his readiness to use *dolos,* cunning, deception, specifically by means of speech, to gain his ends. He has no hesitation about lying for profit. The oracle of Apollo itself had urged *dolos:* deceitful means to a just end. Orestes proves himself full of craft by outlining a lie, a *mythos,* for the Paedagogus to tell.

Orestes' language weaves a network of other allusions to the public life of an Athenian man. He sees himself engaged in the masculine occupation of warfare and pictures himself in competition at the games. He is an adventurer, an exile seeking to recover his patrimony, and virtually a wandering merchant or soldier of fortune; but he is also a vigorous young worker, bread-winner, and man of affairs. His venture is just, we cannot doubt it as he speaks: it is as just as commerce, as just as a prayer for success heeded by gods, as just as battling to win back a homeland. Our favorable impressions of him make us acquiesce in his ethic: a good, gainful end justifies any necessary, sanctioned means.

Orestes' mentality has usually perplexed critics, since he seems without any sensibility at all. He seeks his goal with complete assurance and no scruples, doubts, or passion. We see him lucidly and coolly plotting a venture of life and death. The reason for these peculiarities of "personality" is now clear. Orestes symbolizes a mind that exists only in external action, only for external action, rational and realistic.

The speeches of Orestes and the Paedagogus define more precisely this mentality and the dramatic world inhabited by the men. It is a world of *ergon*—bodily activity, externality, work—in which *logos*—utterance, thought, language—depends on *ergon*—the product, action, fact—for its validity. In these terms Orestes' set-speech contrasts two kinds of *logos:* valid, correlated with *ergon;* and spurious, opposed to it or separated from it. For him and the Paedagogus, meaningful *logoi,* words, statements, further the deed or spring from actualities. *Logoi* of this sort are a prerequisite for effective action because they lead to clarity about the best plan: we see the men using speech in this way in their discussion. In this sense also *logoi* correspond to *erga* as a true proposition or conception corresponds to the way things really are. Such *logoi* can be an instrument of action as well: the essential feature of Orestes' plan is a *mythos* or story for the Paedagogus to tell. Thus *logos* can connote pretense, since it can conceal the true state of affairs though grounded in it. In this vein Orestes draws on the common Greek antithesis of false *logoi* and the *erga* of truth:

> Why should it grieve me, if I die in pretense (*logos*)
> But in reality (*erga*) stay safe . . .

In this way too, Orestes affirms *erga,* since they cannot possibly be inauthentic and since they define the truth and falsehood of *logoi.*

Orestes' language is discursive, orderly, logical; and *logos* for him means prose. He speaks well, but his rhetoric is conventional, that of the public assembly, military strategy, or princely directive.

Orestes' speech as a whole is itself a *logos* corresponding to an *ergon* outside it, the physical action of the drama. For both the speech and the play begin with the Paedagogus; both continue with planning. The phrase, "Let that be the story" (line 50), stands at the exact center of the speech; the Paedagogus' story appears at the exact center of the play. Then Orestes alludes to his reappearance with the urn, then to his "rebirth" to confound his enemies. And, finally, the speech ends, as the play, with the *ergon* of slaying and vengeance.

At the end of the speech the three men prepare to leave the stage. They exit in different directions: the Paedagogus will act by *logoi,* befitting his age or his profession; the younger men, physically. Discussion has served its purpose. The end of their colloquy is the beginning of vengeance.

Through its atmosphere of intrigue and adventure, and by the sheer logic of its development, Orestes' exposition brings us to a full sense of impending action. The exchange between him and his Tutor, then, after a voice moans off-stage, springs from the opposition of *logos* to *ergon* that comes into being when preparations are finished. "Should we wait and listen to the lament?" asks Orestes. "By no means," answers his instructor, "nothing should be set before the necessary actions that will lead us to victory in our task." The rejection here of *logoi* (in the form of *gooi,* cries), for the sake of *erga,* sums up their dramatic world.

When Electra steps from the palace and begins her dirge, we are struck immediately by two things. First, the shift to lyrics, to the free anapests of chanted lamentation, breaks abruptly with the iambics of the preceding dialogue. Second, at the center of the stage we see a lone young woman in place of three men of varying ages. We may now appreciate that these contrasts re-enforce a distinction between a masculine world of *erga,* in which *logoi* are mere servants, and a feminine world of *logoi,* here laments, which preclude physical effectiveness but have another power all their own.

If Orestes is free-ranging, conscienceless, professional, athletic, and businesslike, Electra is tied to the home, unambitious, poverty-stricken, despairing, and frenzied. She stayed behind when Orestes was taken abroad. She is miserable at home because she is treated like a slave. This is her economic condition by contrast to Orestes'. She refuses to seek to better her standard of living. She does not see herself engaged in any public life at all. The palace walls bound her world.

We first hear Electra's voice ringing inside the palace. The Paedagogus stresses its location. When she comes forth through the doors we soon realize that she embodies the interior of that terrible dwelling, her backdrop throughout the play.

Electra's woman's life indoors symbolizes her essential sphere: the internal world of idea, image, and emotion. She grieves in her own bed at night; she locates the source of the family's ills in lust. She is a sensibility laid bare: there is her pity, her hate, and her depression. Orestes plans and acts; Electra suffers and endures. The men confer with one another, within an explicit context of communication. Electra soliloquizes, or rather addresses herself to the elements. She laments: reiterates the memories that haunt her, and dwells on her sufferings. The explicit context of her lament is lamentation itself. A typical one is in progress, and she asserts her intention to repeat the liturgy as long as she lives. Threnody is Electra's occupation, her only mode of action in the sense that Orestes recognized speech as a mode of action. But lamentation is not effectively instrumental, nor does Electra make that claim for it. Viewed as to results, it at best exhorts the spirits of the dead and the nether gods to send Orestes. Her threnody reaches its climax in a cry for her brother. He is to her as he is to himself and the Paedagogus: the requisite avenger of Agamemnon's murder.

Electra's language moves beyond prose. Her threnody is not organized schematically; its imagery evokes unreflecting response. It replaces logic with imaginative *logos* in organic rhythms. Electra's inward universe obliterates distinctions of time and place, and transforms everything tangible into a creature of her own experience.

Whether mourning becomes Electra or not, it has become her life. The thrust toward the future and the suspense built up in us by the schemes of the men recede and vanish. Harmonious exchange of advice has been supplanted by the echo of Electra's voice crying in public solitude, as she vows

> With continual wailing, before paternal doors,
> To utter a resounding cry for all to hear.

Electra's grieving is, in a sense, self-perpetuated; yet it flows from a perception of real horror and torment. Through her eyes we see the murder of Agamemnon, as well as the wretched life that she has led since. She draws us into the domestic torment and tension as we respond to her inwardness, and into her inner torment and tension as we respond to the domestic.

In forcing us to enter her private world, Electra lodges us in an atmosphere that will dominate the play. *Logos* and *ergon* have reversed their relationship, for Electra suffers under *erga*, rather than produces them. Her *logoi* express emotion, rather than plot deeds. Her power lies all in *logos*; physically she is impotent. We are already aware of the tension within *logos* between truth and falsehood. Now we begin to realize that *logos* is an absolute, and in part beyond this distinction.

The Parodos, significantly in the form of a lengthy *kommos* or liturgical lament, turns not on any doubts about the condemnation of the vicious Clytemnestra but on the Chorus' friendly criticism of Electra's excessive talk and mourning. "Why do you continually lament?" the Chorus ask. "Why do you desire to suffer?" The questions and objections of the Chorus concerning Electra's verbal activity evoke the greater part of what she chants. From the outset she accepts the character ascribed to her. She links herself with the fabled singer, the nightingale, and with the perpetually weeping Niobe. She too will persist in rage, frenzy, and "countless threnodies."

The Parodos achieves a remarkable dramatic result. Electra wins our closest sympathy and touchingly defends her stance; at the same time, she exhibits and avows shameful behavior, irrationality, and sheer, self-defeating stubbornness. She defends lament for its own sake, though she grants that it is self-lacerating and self-degrading. She is, by a kind of necessary, heroic obstinacy, at war with herself as well as with her environment. Lamentation and rebuke make up her *ethos*, and this is a habit-and-trait that she feels futile and, in one sense, immoral. She can fully affirm only the righting of a now doubly violated moral order; and this would require an act of vengeance. But, alone, she is able only to mourn and censure the moral disorder, thus further separating herself from the wholly valid. Electra acts under a necessity more profound than moral "principles"; enduring her own conflict while facing her environment manifests her peculiar moral intuition. Her heroism, in other words, as it claims our sympathy in the theater, must express itself in contradiction. We must identify *logos* with this paradoxical intuition.

In part, Electra endures the inherent duality of *logos*: a meaningful activity and a mere substitute for action. Her *logoi* spring from *erga* that have impinged on her, that oppress her now, over which she has no control, and against which her only weapon is speech. On the other hand, her *logoi* possess the autonomy and literally incalculable power of lyric and liturgy.

> I am ashamed, ladies, if I seem to you
> To grieve too much with many threnodies.
> But violence forces me to do them.

Beginning her first set-speech in this vein, Electra assents to the whole drift of the Chorus in the Parodos. She is trapped in a woman's world of polemic and lament. In entering her world of *logoi*, we enter on a series of scenes made up precisely of oratory, polemic, and lament. The issues intrinsic to the distinction of *logos* and *ergon* are debated, implicitly and explicitly, in scenes that advance the physical action, the external plot, hardly at all. These scenes are equally portraits, trials, and punishments. But, passing through these scenes, Electra advances, still within the dilemmas of isolated *logos*, to a recognition of the necessity for external *ergon*. Then the final episodes in the drama present effective action more than they debate issues; Electra becomes Orestes' colleague and subordinates herself to the necessities of vengeance. Yet the heart of the *Electra* remains Electra in isolation and *logos* divorced from *ergon*, not only because of quantitative proportions but because this tragic Electra moves us as the melodramatic Electra cannot. And we recognize that, in the central scenes, *logos* justifies itself in a way that survives the apparent triumph of *ergon* in the finale. In spite of all our preconceptions about the sanctity of literal truth and the urgency of efficient action, in spite of Electra's own acceptance of the correlation of *logos* and *ergon* as Orestes expressed it in the Prologue, the *Electra* shows *logos* omnipotent in its character of faith, ideal, and imaginative language.

The ostensible issue in the first encounter of the two sisters is how one should live, and what one should do, in evil circumstances. But these questions of action are turned into questions about what one should say, believe, and rely on, and the point of the scene virtually becomes Electra's oral forcefulness. The persuasive force of her arguments contains her moral supremacy, as it comes across to us in the theater; her directives as to what Chrysothemis should do (and not do) finally prevail. Though Electra boasts of active resistance, we discover that her accomplishment remains wholly verbal. The ironical result of the scene is that only poor Chrysothemis must actually run a risk, in disobeying her mother and offering a substitute sacrifice to her father.

In the first part of the scene, both sisters show much contempt for mere *logoi*, and both attempt to prove that the other lives by *logos* rather than by *ergon*. Chrysothemis' opening words challenge Electra's futile talk and futile passion (lines 328-31). Chrysothemis then charges that Electra only *seems* to be doing something, while really she harms no one, effects no result. Electra then claims that *she* has been the one engaged in *erga* (l. 350). Chrysothemis has hated their common enemies merely in speech, or "in pretence," while "in reality," "in truth," living comfortably with them (*men logo/ergo de*, ll. 357-58).

To Electra's brilliant dialectical defense of her mode of life by contrast to her sister's, Chrysothemis makes no reply whatsoever, but brushes the whole speech and all its arguments aside by saying to the Chorus: "I am quite used to her talk (*muthon*, l. 373)." And she simply turns to another topic, which proves to be the plan of Clytemnestra and Aegisthus for silencing Electra's "great groans," *ton makron goon* (l. 375), a phrase suggesting *hoi makroi logoi*, "long or over-long speeches," which we shall hear more than once in connection with Electra later in the play. The antithesis of this latter phrase, in fact, occurs a few moments later, when Electra asks for a report of Clytemnestra's dream.

> *Chrysothemis.* Do these night terrors make you hopeful?
> *Electra.* If you told me the vision, then I might say.
> *Chrysothemis.* But I know only very little to tell.
> *Electra.* Then say *that*. A few words (*logoi*) have often
> Overthrown or re-established men.
> *Chrysothemis.* The story is. . . . (The *logos* is. . . .)

These lines might be said to speak for themselves. Electra's gnomic pronouncement about the power of "a few words," *smikroi logoi*, deserves amplification, however. These *logoi* are at once instrumental, instructive, and potent in themselves. Her defense of *logoi* as autonomous forces in human life coheres with her own reliance on the ritual *logoi* of lament, the competitive *logoi* of persuasion and self-defense, and the battling *logoi* of reproach and insult.

The debate ends with Chrysothemis persuaded to do as Electra oids.

> *Chrysothemis.* I will do it. It is not reasonable for two people
> To dispute what is just, but rather to hasten to do it.

She contrasts the fruitless *logoi* of dispute with daring action (*to dran* and *ton ergon*). Then she begs for silence, the necessary companion of a successful venture. We shall meet this corollary of the basic duality again later. We may notice here that the colloquy between the sisters ends with the commencement of a deed, as at the exit of the three partners in the Prologue. The silence of the interlocutors thus has positive dramatic effect.

Clytemnestra enters with attendants bearing ritual offerings such as Chrysothemis had carried in the previous Episode. In their first words both mother and sister rebuke Electra for again being outside the palace talking. In both scenes Electra proves stronger; here she convicts her mother of criminal guilt. For it is a case of murder; or, rather, there are two murders, Iphigeneia's and Agamemnon's. Electra acts as prosecutor against her mother, and as lawyer for the defense of her father. The language of the interchange seats us in the law-courts. And the whole scene ultimately turns not so much on questions of substantive justice as on an examination of the debating process and of the use of speech as a mode of action.

Were we not attuned to the issue of *logos* and *ergon,* it would be hard to understand why the most violent exchange in this most violent scene uses such abstruse language.

> *Electra.*   Shameful deeds are taught by shameful deeds.
> *Clytemnestra.*   O shameless creature, I and my words
> And my deeds make you say much too much.
> *Electra.*   *You* say it, not I. For you do
> The deed; and deeds find words for themselves.
> *Clytemnestra.*   By Lady Artemis, you"ll pay for this impudence . . .

Clytemnestra's pairing of words and deeds, implying the sum total of behavior, contrasts to Electra's sole activity, talk. The phrase, "make you say too much," *agan legein poei,* presents the central duality in miniature. Electra's paradoxical reply, *"You* say it," attempts to justify her talk by pleading the compulsion of deeds. "You do the deed," she says, *su gar poeis/tourgon,* implying not only that Clytemnestra is her antithesis (as *ergon versus* her *logos*), but that deeds or circumstances produce speech.

"Deeds find words for themselves": *ta d'erga tous logous heurisketai.* Electra's ultimate line of self-defense implies that words are subservient to deeds, as passive to active, or as effect to cause. Thus she expresses the ambiguous autonomy of *logos* and of her own character in the face of *erga.* The debate between mother and daughter quite literally consists of words sprung inevitably from foul deeds. The next scene presents words necessitated by a just enterprise. In a sense not intended by Electra, "deeds find words for themselves" implies that deeds require *logoi* as means, and hence that the deed afoot, Orestes', will call forth the *mythos* of the Paedagogus. Thus the proposition serves as a transition in the theater.

The Paedagogus' false account of Orestes' death (the longest set-speech in the extant work of Sophocles) complements Clytemnestra's self-convicting prayer, and, by eye-for-eye justice, gives her what she deserves. But the *mythos*, which we have been expecting since Orestes outlined its plot in the Prologue, also complements Electra's verbal virtuosity. Her character, with its essentially monochromatic reliance on verbal action, and its duality of pathos and power, leaps to accept the Paedagogus' story in its shattering ramifications. Her suffering is real, and affects us. But we realize at the same time that it is consonant with her character to be taken in by a verbal stratagem, by verbal seeming. Clytemnestra says that *she* will wait for the ashes, as proof of the story. But Electra interrupts and pushes away the Chorus' suggestions about hope for Orestes' life. The succeeding scene will show Electra rejecting even concrete evidence on the question of the alleged death, and able in her turn to give a plausible explanation (*logos*) for Chrysothemis' discoveries. Electra shows a stubborn refusal to doubt the worst; an immense capacity to endow thought with reality.

The Paedagogus' speech stands dead-center in the play. It is not without significance that both the plan of Orestes and the total action of the drama pivot on this unrivaled exhibition of verbal verisimilitude. For us as audience, the speech flows naturally as part of the original scheme. But now the story has another level of impact on us. It completes the pathos of Electra; the compulsion behind her suffering as she listens proves its noble strength. The *mythos* becomes an *ergon* tormenting her.

The Paedagogus' speech deploys the power in *logoi*, just as Electra had in persuasive colloquy with Chrysothemis or in her admirable prosecution of Clytemnestra. And, in the Paedagogus' speech shines again the double nature of *logos*. The speech is instrumental, valid, justified, and effective, in the strategy of revenge; it is deceiving, spurious, and grievous in its immediate effects. We marvel at the persuasiveness of a story which we know is false. We suffer with Electra though we know that she will eventually rejoice. Because the lie completes Electra's pathos, her transformation begins. In despair she finds new determination. For the first time in the play she makes a decision to act physically. The second confrontation between the sisters contrasts at many points with the first, emphasizing Electra's new attitude. Before, she had succeeded in persuading Chrysothemis to do something, however minimal, by way of rebellion; here, she fails to persuade, but vows she stands ready to act alone. She abandons the effort at persuasion. But, at the end of the scene, Electra does not depart. Chrysothemis she sends away, remaining on stage during the second Stasimon. For after all, we reflect, Orestes will come, has come; and Electra will never do the deed.

There is, in fact, similar irony throughout the second meeting of the sisters. Electra defends the deed that she proposes by stressing the good repute, *logon eukleia,* that will accrue. Again and again she argues from what others will say, quoting finally an imaginary eulogy at length. These rather suspect forms of reputation, spun out into a fable with a happy ending, contrast with the honor, accompanied by lands and rule, which Orestes seeks. The scene as a whole impresses us once again with the schism in Electra's stance. She would venture on deeds in pursuit of kind words.

The same schism lies behind the dispute over the tokens. Electra presents herself to Chrysothemis as tough-minded, and claims to judge by the way things are rather than by private opinions. She accuses her sister of being deceived by words.

> *Electra.* Alas! Who told you this story (*logos*)
> That you believe in all too fully?

Chrysothemis argues that her "hypothesis" is warranted by clear evidence.

> *Chrysothemis.* I saw clear signs for myself,
> And do not believe another's story.

The irony of Electra's position in this interchange is patent. So it is also in her last exhibition of persuasive force, when she counters

Chrysothemis' self-conscious deduction from the tokens to Orestes' presence (lines 907-15) with her own evidence, mere hearsay.

> *Chrysothemis.*   Alas! Who told you these things?
> *Electra.*   The man nearest when he died.

For us, the plausibility of her explanation of the tokens hardly belies its pathetic spuriousness. However, while Chrysothemis had shown a merely logical skill, Electra's moral and emotional force carries the day. This dispute, then, exposes the deceitfulness of *logoi* (words, arguments, reasons) when divorced from *erga* (acts, facts, things), but simultaneously exhibits the potency of autonomous *logos* (conviction, imagination, inwardness). If Electra reaches her largest heroic stature in this scene, it can only be because her force and her folly unite in her essential commitment to pure *logos*, and only because *logos* itself possesses an authenticity beyond the judgment of reason and the world. Here *logos* completely triumphs over logic.

Since Orestes and Electra are living emblems of the play's basic conceptual duality, in the "recognition" scene visible dramatic effects stand out, corresponding to their physical reunion. Orestes enters carrying an urn. This urn, like a third actor, dominates the stage until the final minute of the dialogue. It is the reason given for the stranger's presence; Electra cries out at the sight of it, and, holding it in her arms, addresses it in a long and moving lament; finally, Orestes tries to recover it from her, and his explanation of who he is revolves around explaining what the urn is not.

> *Orestes.*   Give up this urn then, so you may learn all.

For the urn is a surrogate Orestes, an Orestes by sham, a fiction posing as fact. What Electra and we alike "recognize" in the scene is a distinction between reality and supposition, between expectation and event, between true and false evidence.

In fact, something similar happens to Orestes as well. He suffers in seeing (and hearing) Electra's suffering, and alters his course of action. As he replaces concealment through silence with revelatory speech, Electra replaces her compelling though misdirected lamentation with joy. From this mutual shift results the sweetness of the climactic moments: Electra releases the urn (line 1217), soon to take Orestes himself in her arms (line 1225). Orestes with one hand shows Electra the ring that proves what the urn that he holds in the other had only shammed. At the end of the dialogue, the urn recedes from the level of personage to that of mere object, and all our attention rests on the living pair.

But speech plays a major role in this scene alongside the urn. Electra's lament overpowers us; and it overpowers Orestes. At its conclusion he finds himself at a loss for words:

> Woe, woe, what shall I say? So perplexed,
> Where can I go in speech? I no longer have the strength
>   to control my tongue.

For the first time in the play, Orestes suffers under the force of evils from without. Thus he shares, at least momentarily, his sister's trait of compulsive speech and also her relationship to *erga kaka*. At their moment of reunion Orestes enters the world of Electra, just as she had already gone far toward entering his in the preceding scene. For this reason, contrary to plan, Orestes admits his former lie, saying that the urn is "not Orestes, except tricked out in speech (logo)."

The mutual recognition of brother and sister, and their experience of self-recognition, achieve a fragile resolution of conflict in this scene. But it lasts only a moment. We then plunge back into tension between talk and the deed at hand which pulls apart the newly joined couple.

The seeming duet between Electra and Orestes (lines 1232-87) actually shows no harmonizing at all. For Orestes does not join in; he has no lyric lines, only the rational iambics of discourse. We see dramatized again, in fact, the contrast so striking in the Prologue, between Electra's threnody, here reversed to exaltation, and Orestes' controlled deliberations. Orestes' constant effort is to terminate this "duet." We have forced on us again an awareness that a violent endeavor, demanding secrecy, is in progress, and that talk may give everything away and bring disaster.

The scene between the song and the short third Stasimon serves as a vital transition to the so-called Exodos, which is the climax of the action. The transition involves a gradual alteration in the attitude of Electra; and a few more, final touches in the education

of Orestes, supplied by the Paedagogus. The scene takes us closer
to the means and the end represented by the Paedagogus, and
more fully into his world of *ergon*.

At the beginning of the dialogue Orestes puts his attitude toward
Electra's melic interlude as vigorously and as bluntly as possible:
"Cease all superfluous speech" (line 1288). In a coherent, concise
statement, built around a rhetorical opposition of *logos* to *ergon*, he
requests Electra not to waste precious time with a recapitulation of
the past. "For," he says, "talk (*logos*) would hinder the moment of
opportunity (*kairos*)" (line 1292). In a gracious though roundabout
reply, Electra agrees to cooperate, and gives him the facts that he
needs to know. She thus explicitly recognizes the urgent require-
ments of the situation.

The Paedagogus' outburst, as he reenters, puts more strongly
what we ourselves feel increasingly: the crucial act can wait no
longer. He denounces both brother and sister because they could
have been overheard inside if he had not been on guard. The conclusion of his speech sums up the dramatic moment as we experience
it in terms of the necessity to put talk aside.

> Now cease your long speeches
> And your insatiate cries of joy.
> Go in: in these circumstances, delay
> Means ruin, but the time is right for success.

But there is more delay, as Electra recognizes the old man and
realizes that he had "killed her with lies (*logois*), while knowing the
sweetest truths (*erga*)." Then, with his last words in the play, the
Paedagogus calls on the concepts crucial to his first speech in the
Prologue, *kairos* and *ergon*. From now to the end of the drama, he
remains silent, because the action moves ahead on schedule. After
Orestes transmits a final directive to his partner,

> We have no more need of long speeches,
> But only of getting inside as quickly as possible,

the men perform the ritual reverences preparatory to the sanctified
slaying, and leave the stage in silence. As her part in the venture,
Electra offers a prayer to Apollo. It contains suggestions that this
verbal ritual is her best aid.

In this transitional scene, therefore, Electra begins to share the men's view of speech as an accompaniment to silent endeavor. In the concluding minutes of the play, she will turn her formidable verbal powers into instruments of vengeance: by reporting what happens; by deceiving Aegisthus; and by crucial exhortations to action.

At the outset, the final scene gives us two surprises: Electra leaves the stage for the first time since she entered in the Prologue; and, in the *kommos*, she has no lyrics, but leaves them all to the Chorus. Her first words convey the change that has occurred:

> Dear ladies, now in a moment the men
> Will finish their work. Wait in silence.

This directive to the Chorus repeats almost word for word Orestes' first objection to her joyous song (line 1236). Her alliance is now with *tourgon* and she realizes that it requires silence. She re-enters, she tells the Chorus, to serve as lookout: she is on stage to *do* something. Then Clytemnestra's death-cries bespeak the effectiveness of Orestes. Electra encourages him to strike again. Indeed, what we see and what we hear at the moment of matricide make Electra the dramatic agent of vengeance. It is as though her shouts were swords.

Next, Electra deals with Aegisthus, in a masterpiece of *double entendre*, telling the truth and deceiving at the same time. Previously we have seen Electra in the reverse position, the victim of a lie. At other times she was unable to distinguish between literal truth and literal falsity. Now that she knows how things stand, she employs her wit to keep us constantly aware that she knows, while lulling Aegisthus to ignorance of his danger.

> *Aegisthus.* Where might the strangers be? Tell me that.
> *Electra.* Inside. They have reached a kind hostess.

Here Electra's verb, *katenusan*, means not only "they have reached the house," but "they have accomplished the murder" of their "hostess." In this way, Electra proves her talent for *dolos* of a sort even more highly refined than the men's. Similarly, in the next exchange,

> *Aegisthus.* And did they genuinely report his death?
> *Electra.* No, they have brought himself, not news alone.

Evidence and hearsay, truth and falsity, Electra plays on these
ground-themes while sustaining ambiguity perfectly.

Clytemnestra's body under the sheet plays the same part as
Orestes' urn: both serve as pivots for a reversal from delusion to
truth. "Alas, I understand your word. It is Orestes speaking to me"
(lines 1479-80); Aegisthus recognizes Orestes by what he says. This
transition from the dead mother to the living son, and from sight
back to speech, shifts our attention to the dialogue itself and prepares us for the climax of the role of Electra, as she interrupts the
desperate attempt of Aegisthus to stall for time:

> *Aegisthus.*   Just let me say a little bit.
> *Electra.*   Don't let him say any more!
>   By the gods, brother, do not prolong speeches.
>   What profit can delay bring, when a man
>   In the midst of trouble is about to die?

Her rejection of talk, of "long speeches," here, in favor of pressing
speedily toward the deed and the profit, completes her evolution into
an effective ally for Orestes in the vengeance.

Just as Electra alters in her relation to *logoi*, so she will no
longer remain crushed by *erga*. Aegisthus' instant death will relieve
her. Her final words in the play encourage her brother in the
style of the Paedagogus (though Orestes needs little chiding), adding
a bitter sense of intolerable *kaka* all her own. Only by full requital
of the extreme *kaka* under which she has suffered can she find
release; thus she demands the harshest treatment for Aegisthus'
body.

Orestes pushes Aegisthus inside, the concluding exit-for-action
of the drama, leaving us with a statement of his attitude toward requital. Illegal or foul deeds beget just deeds as punishment, even
if these just deeds mean murder. He is still firm in his belief
that by the appropriate *ergon* we can diminish *to panourgon*, evil-
doing. To this end, in silence Orestes and Aegisthus enter the
palace; Electra watches in silence.

Thus the *Electra* plays out the dialectic of *logos* and *ergon* and
presents Electra first and foremost in her relationship to these two
principles. Throughout the play her temper remains constant, as

does her reliance on *logoi*; yet her final attitude, for all practical purposes, is equivalent to that of Orestes in the Prologue. But what is our final attitude toward her? The last utterances of Orestes and Electra each show fully their characteristic mentalities: his legalistic, simplistic efficiency; her passionate, urgent absolutism. "Kill all wrongdoers"; "Throw him to the fitting buriers." And so, despite her evolving determination to act, Electra remains essentially the same from beginning to end. And so also our response to her in the Exodos or finale remains as it has been throughout, divided between admiration and disquiet. Yet, like *logos* and *ergon* and the other antitheses of the play, admiration and disquiet are incommensurable in the theater: Electra carries us away beyond criticism. In the lament over the urn, in the *kommoi* and the songs of joy, she retains the power that encounters us in her opening *threnos*. This is the power of *logos*. It draws us to the end.

Since the essential autonomy of his protagonist lasts as long as the play, Sophocles affirms a necessity beyond the practical and "realistic" necessity for the coordination of *logos* and *ergon* that we see in the Exodos. This other, higher necessity is that implied by spiritual *logos* in isolation from worldliness. The schism we notice within Electra and within her world dramatizes the contrast between a *logos* more profound than logic and a *logos* defined wholly in terms of external *ergon*. It is this latter *logos* alone that Orestes uses. By the end of the play Electra has shown some capacity to include the calculating, "rational" *logos* within her primarily emotional, intuitive, and imaginative *logos*. Thus again we find her bursting beyond the balance of opposites into a more capacious wholeness.

Electra dominates the other characters and the drama as a whole because she commands a language moving beyond logic. We recognize her nobility and strength most fully during the very moments in which she fails most pathetically to grasp *ergon* (facts, evidence, material reality). When she is in error about the tokens, deceived by the Paedagogus' lie, or deluded about the urn, she surges forth, deciding to act alone, enduring the torments of despair, lyrically overwhelming us with noble grief. In this way, each scene from her threnody on shows Electra's spiritual *logos* in tension with the demands of fact and deed. But this state of tension too is imbalanced. Its constant ironical undertone cannot counteract our attachment to Electra's truth. The tension only serves to bring into the light the essence of her truth: paradox. The paradox of Electra informs each scene; she so transcends ordinary logic that she draws our sympathies most when least reasonable.

The opening and closing of our play both show the world of *ergon* ostensibly dominant; both present the men in control, and support their world conceptually as well as dramatically. The large center of the play criticizes the world of *logos;* its keystone is the great speech of the Paedagogus, at the exact middle. With this structure, the *Electra* asserts the practical and literal truth of *ergon,* but also, shattering this frame, the uncanny force of *logos.* In the center, speeches, lyrics, and faith prove more authoritative than deeds, and Electra holds sway in a rhythmic world of meaningful pathos, ritual, and chant.

Because the center shatters its frame, the finale does not simply balance the beginning in abstract symmetry. It is not the same un-ambiguous melodrama, but sardonic and tense. And, while validating the men's purpose, it vindicates an Electra who remains self-con-tradictory. Her vindication, even her redemption, leaves us with unresolved issues, permanent paradoxes: the role of her thrust toward infinity in a finite world, the fate of her ideals in the midst of actuality. Forever intersecting and separating, these incommen-surables are somehow, beyond our understanding, related. The limits of our understanding, after all, are those of logic in the face of *logos.* That the incommensurables are truly related, however, the play proves in its own perfect union of deed and word, real and ideal.

Silence, as we have noticed, has a positive dramatic function in the *Electra.* From her entrance on, Electra stands silent during only three periods of any length: the first two Stasima and the *mythos* of the Paedagogus. We appreciate well the force of the Paedagogus' speech and its relevance to Electra's symbolic character. The two choral odes, in a similar way, also derive an important part of their force and significance from Electra. The Chorus not only speaks in her favor but hardly exists at all in this drama except as an adjunct to her; always subordinate, always a helpful backdrop for her attitudes, merits, emotions, pathos. In the only two developed choral odes, then, I suggest that the Chorus remains an extension of Electra's character and continues to bring it out and augment it: the Chorus represents her participation in the communal *logoi* of ritual. Electra can willingly stand silent on stage during these odes because the Chorus acts out, in lyric and dance, her own dedication to the liturgical truths of tradition, inwardness, and faith. As at the very end of the drama, Electra's silence displays assent, communion, and assurance; justice will prevail, it implies; divinities are working invisible like words.

This essay can only suggest in conclusion that the *Electra*, like its heroine, takes on its most profound dimension by uniting *logos* and *mythos* (terms used interchangeably throughout). For the men the prime example of *mythos* or *logos* is no doubt the well-wrought scheme or lie. For Electra, however, the *logoi* or *mythoi* imitate and exemplify the ebb and flow of nature itself. The cycles of nature—nature's rituals—like the seasons, life and death, or night and day, form *logoi* or *mythoi* (meaningful patterns), just as they form the basis of human ritual and of the traditional myths. Electra symbolizes *physis*, nature, in her endurance, her attachment to blood, her repetitions, and her refusal to compromise. Electra's truth (and her meaning), like that of nature, is beyond appearances, the surface truths or *erga* apprehended by the senses or sensible intelligence. The appearances are indeed against her; but only the appearances.

Ergon vs. logos, appearance *vs. physis*, fact *vs.* faith: Sophocles captures these great *agones* or conflicts by dramatizing them in perpetual motion, by imitating them for all time in a ritual drama in which the *agonistoi* or competitors play out their war over and over, the struggle without end, the whole ordered and stable. He triumphs by integrating dramatic *erga* and *logoi*, realism, fiction, and rite. But *logoi* and *mythoi* themselves triumph, by expressing the essence of the drama. And our access, such as it is, to this drama is also through *logos* and *mythos*: imagination allowing us to participate in another world.

Apocalypse: *Oedipus at Colonus*

by Cedric H. Whitman

The *Philoctetes* contains the key to Sophocles' late period and throws light backward to the *Electra* and forward to the *Oedipus at Colonus*. It is often said that Sophocles in his later years showed the influence of Euripides in that he began to stage beggared kings and heroes in rags as his protagonists. But the merely theatrical aspects explain little. What Sophocles saw in these crownless and shattered figures was the everlasting contradiction of inner and outer value. It is hard to see how the supremacy of man's inner divinity could have achieved fuller expression than in the shimmering vision of Heracles. And yet, even there the poet had been forced to introduce a divine character who was, technically at least, outside the plot. He was still to some extent bound by the old form of bringing the gods to man, though his real meaning was to raise the god within man to the dignity of a legitimate and recognized universal.

In the *Oedipus at Colonus,* there is no *deus ex machina* in any sense. Everything appears through the man himself, and from the messenger who relates his last hour. The understanding of a certain heroic, albeit paradoxical, supremacy attainable within the scheme of time, and itself constituting a kind of victory over time, grew steadily in the *Philoctetes* from a dim intuitive force into clear religious knowledge. Oedipus, beginning with that knowledge, now becomes a god—in the specifically fifth-century sense of a god such as man can become. His anguished burden of tragic courage has by its

very weight prevented him from turning into the shadow the gods
would make of him; for his tragic courage is as divine and inviolable
as they. The gods are shattering truth, but they are also moral
perception and inner law. Herein, therefore, in the transfiguration
of Oedipus, "deep calleth unto deep," and the gods meet. It is with
a strange ambivalence, in his enormous strength and utter helplessness, guided at once by his oracular soul and by a frail girl, that
Oedipus comes once more upon the stage.

The *Oedipus at Colonus*, it has often been observed, lacks the
daemonic *élan* of the other two Theban plays; it contains less obvious conflict, save what is concentrated in the scenes with Creon and
Polyneices. But in Sophoclean tragedy, action may be defined as the
functioning of the hero's will, in whatever form. Since all his heroes
exercise will, it follows that there are no so-called "passive" protagonists. The *Oedipus at Colonus* does not lack action, for the will of
Oedipus functions steadily with great power and effect; but there is
one element of heroic action which is absent for the first time in the
extant works of Sophocles. That is the element of self-destructive-
ness which hitherto inevitably accompanied the operation of the
hero's will. Even in the late works, where self-preservation plays so
important a part, the conditions of self-preservation are sufficiently
rigorous so that, in order to preserve integrity, the hero may choose
rather to destroy himself, as Philoctetes does at first, or risk almost
inevitable death, as Electra does when she elects to slay the tyrants
herself. But Oedipus is beyond all such choices and risks. He would
not be what he is, the most exalted of Sophocles' heroes, if he still
had to achieve his height by self-destruction; he has been destroyed
enough, and his tlemosyne is complete. If victory costs him little,
that is because life has already cost him so much. Action, insofar
as it means simply the functioning of the heroic will, is present in
dynamic abundance. But the struggles which had been deadly in
earlier works appear now in a diminutive and fine focus; their
issues are settled before they take place. All is still passionately felt,
but more through the distilled medium of the intellect than directly through experience—a fact in itself appropriate to Oedipus,
who had put faith in the intellect from the first.

The *Oedipus at Colonus* is a folk tale, a mystery play, and a national festival piece, the essential elements of whose plot may have

belonged to the mythology attached to the hero-cult, though certainly not to the oldest form of the myth. Aeschylus in the *Seven against Thebes* dramatized the consequences of the curse which caused the sons of Oedipus to "divide their inheritance with the sword," and the poets of the Theban cycle knew of the curse; but in both the *Iliad* and the *Odyssey*, Oedipus is supposed to have remained king of Thebes, even after his self-discovery, until he died. Sophocles' account of how he came to the Athenian suburb of Colonus as a wanderer, underwent deification, and subsequently was worshipped, seemed to Pausanias doubtful, since it conflicted with Homer's version. Therefore the great archaeologist made inquiries, and learned still another story, that the bones of Oedipus had been brought to Colonus after his death. Yet Sophocles did not invent his story, for Euripides alludes to it in the *Phoenissae* of 409 in a way that would have been incomprehensible if the tradition were not common knowledge. And two years before, when the Athenians won a slight cavalry skirmish over the Thebans near Acharnae, which is not far from Colonus, the credit for the victory had been accorded to the deified Oedipus. Neither Euripides nor Sophocles therefore can be the source of the tale. What is perhaps likely, though quite hypothetical, is that during the fifth century the tide of Athenian nationalism found religious expression not only in the monuments of the new age which were rising on the Acropolis, but equally in a revival of interest in the chthonian cults of the old Attic heroes, of which the greatest was Theseus. His bones were recovered from the island of Scyros in 473 by Cimon. If, as Pausanias seems to have found out, there actually was a similar "recovery" of the bones of Oedipus, the growth of such a story as Sophocles tells would be an almost indispensable means for explaining Oedipus' otherwise feeble connections with Attica. In any case, there he was, sharing his shrine at Colonus with Theseus, Pirithous, and Adrastus.

The plot which Sophocles presents fits smoothly into the *Oedipus Rex*. Not all the intervening events are told, but it is significant that Oedipus is now in exile, not of his own free will, but because he has been ejected from Thebes by the new ruler Creon, while his two sons, Polyneices and Eteocles, did nothing to help him. When the first of his shock and fury was past, Oedipus had thought better of his wish for death or exile. Even in Thebes his extraordinary resilience had partially restored him to his belief in himself, so that he was content to live his life out among his children. Not until then had his masters decided to drive him out. Much time has passed; Oedipus is now old, and Antigone, who was a little girl in the *Oedipus Rex,* is fully grown and able to accompany her father's wanderings.

The prologue, like all Sophoclean prologues, introduces not only the matter but also the spirit of the play. As Deianeira's monologue suits her peculiar isolation, or the clean-limbed issues of the *Antigone* are first symbolized in the formal, balanced contrasts of the opening scene, so the last two plays, where quiet deliverance after pain and true insights of inner value are the aims, have prologues where people enter searching, either on an unfamiliar island or at the fringes of an unknown city. Oedipus enters searching for a world in which the value that he has set upon himself through years of suffering may be acknowledged as true. Alone at first with Antigone, he enters the outskirts of Athens and asks where he is. Not recognizing the place, Antigone gazes about her and says:

> Straight ahead
> I can perceive towers that crown a city:
> And it is safe to guess, this place is holy,
> Teeming with laurel, olive, and the vine;
> Within the grove itself, the nightingales
> In numbers sing.

Shortly a stranger enters who, shocked to see that the old man has seated himself on a sacred stone, will answer no questions till Oedipus moves. He then tells them that they are in Athens, the realm of Theseus, and more specifically in the sacred grove of the Eumenides in the deme of Colonus. Oedipus wishes to see the king at once; he says he has come to perform a great service. But the stranger begs him to stay where he is until he can fetch some of his fellows to decide whether Oedipus is to be allowed to remain or not. Oedipus waits patiently, and prays meanwhile to the dread goddesses to pity "this wretched shadow of Oedipus." But he has already won a sign of respect. Before he leaves, the stranger remarks that he seems noble, "save for what the gods have done to him."

The people of Colonus now enter as chorus and question the wanderer further. They note his blindness, grow increasingly suspicious, and finally wring from him that he is Oedipus. In horror they order him to leave at once, lest he bring his guilt and pollution on the city. Oedipus defends himself vigorously, and the chorus, pitying him, agrees that Theseus must decide. A woman is now seen approaching on horseback. Antigone recognizes her as her sister Ismene, who has come to warn Oedipus of his danger. The latter manifests no surprise when he hears that a war for the throne of Thebes has broken out between his two sons, Eteocles and Polyneices. The combatants have need of Oedipus, for they have heard a prophecy that whichever side is favored by Oedipus' presence will be victorious, and Eteocles, the present ruler of Thebes, is sending the ex-regent Creon to fetch Oedipus home. The Thebans, however, have no intention of risking the presence of a polluted parricide within their walls; they merely want him near by, where he can be useful; but he is not to be reinstated in his home. Oedipus listens grimly and then with bitter words swears that neither of his sons shall have help from him. He will remain at Athens.

A lyric scene follows, in which Oedipus makes his peace with the Eumenides for having trespassed in their grove, and presently Theseus enters. All action halts as the two great men confront each other. During the whole scene, Antigone is silent, and the chorus makes only one shy interruption. The king's address is notable for its broad humanism:

> I myself was reared in exile
> Like you, and the perils of a foreign land
> I bore in my own person on my head.
> Wherefore I should be loath to fail assisting
> An exile, like yourself, a nothingness.
> For being a man, I know I have no share
> Of tomorrow which is greater than your own.

Oedipus comes immediately to the point. He craves burial in Attica and has brought his own body to Theseus as a gift. These lines are only comprehensible, of course, in the context of the heroic cults of the dead. In order to receive any benefit from a hero, one had to possess his bones. The dead man was thus a chthonian divinity whose remains, albeit buried, performed a lively service of protection throughout a relatively small region. Greece was full of such heroic graves. The chthonian religion connected with them was much older than the Olympian hierarchy, and it seems to have suffered no comparable loss of belief in the fifth century, or even much later. Tombs of nameless heroes were carefully tended in Greece long after the Parthenon became a museum. Oedipus was, therefore, offering Theseus a real blessing in the form of his corpse, for both are perfectly aware that Oedipus is a heroic personage. The only surprising thing is that Oedipus can consider himself a hero before he is dead. This fact only emphasizes Sophocles' concern with the heroic nature, and how it comes to be. The mere superstition about dead bones is not enough for him.

Oedipus now leads the conversation around to the approaching war, and here again Sophocles does a characteristic thing. He deliberately confuses the prophecy. Ismene has reported from Delphi that Oedipus will be useful in the war threatening between Eteocles and Polyneices; Oedipus now prophesies that his body will be useful in the coming war between Thebes and Athens. Theseus in some surprise asks what will cause war to break out with this friendly power, and Oedipus, in a splendid speech, lays the cause at the door of time:

> O dearest son of Aegeus, for the gods
> Alone it is to feel nor age nor death:
> All other things almighty time confounds.
> The strength of the earth wanes, the body wanes,
> Faith dies and falsehood blossoms in its place,
> And so in men the spirit does not rest
> The same, either in cities or in friends.
> For some today, for others not long after
> Sweet turns to bitter, and again to sweet,
> And if today the weather's fair twixt Thebes
> And you, no less does countless time in passage
> Breed on and on his countless nights and days,
> Wherein your present bonds of harmony
> Shall scatter at the spear's point, for a word:
> And there my sleeping and long-buried corpse
> Cold in the earth shall drink their hot blood down,
> If Zeus be Zeus, and his Apollo true.

Thus in his own person Oedipus prophesies; but his words tell only what his own action shall bring about. Like the gods, who "feel nor age nor death," he can already speak from outside time. This prophecy is, like all the others in Sophocles, symbolic, not causal, and of greater significance to the character of the hero than to the plot. Theseus is impressed at once by the authority of the old man's manner and promises him not only burial in Attica, but also full protection and citizenship. He may even come and live in Theseus' own house, so little does the prince fear ritual pollution. But Oedipus declines, saying he is now on the spot where he will conquer those who have exiled him. Theseus then, with a few last words of reassurance, retires, and the chorus brings the first great section of the play to a close with one of the most exquisite lyrics to be found in Greek tragedy, the famous ode on Athens.

From the first moment of his arrival, Oedipus has put down roots in Attica; he has begun to assert a spiritual authority over his environment. Blind and beggarly as he is, he is nevertheless irresistible. The next section, or act, of the play shows Oedipus' struggle to defend his new position. First Creon arrives from Thebes and attempts to win Oedipus' support in the impending contest. He begins with a specious pretense of pity for Oedipus' sufferings and says he has come to take him home. Oedipus denounces him roundly. Creon then resorts to force, abducts both Ismene and Antigone and tries to drag away Oedipus himself. His attempt is balked by Theseus, however, who leads out his soldiers, rescues the girls, and sends Creon off with a lecture on manners. Creon's answer is a declaration of war, and he departs.

Polyneices, the elder son of Oedipus, is now reported near. Oedipus at first refuses to see him, but finally agrees to do so, on the intercession of Antigone. In a long and moving appeal, Polyneices confesses his negligence and begs forgiveness and assistance. He wears the look of a man blasted and going to his doom. Unquestionably sincere both in his need and his remorse, he has come to Oedipus as a last hope to avert the destruction he feels overhanging the seven champions who are to attack Thebes. Oedipus is silent for a long time; then his answer comes in the form of one of the most inspired and daemonic execrations ever pronounced. He curses not only Polyneices, but Eteocles also, and offers not the slightest word of comfort or farewell. Shattered, Polyneices takes a sorrowful leave of Antigone; she begs him to abandon the expedition, but he feels his duty as a leader and returns to his forces.

These two scenes have caused much difficulty. They seem somewhat extraneous and, in the eyes of many, give the work a quality of melodramatic pastiche. Creon's abduction of Antigone and Ismene, for instance, and their rescue by Theseus may seem more at home in a medieval chivalric romance than in an otherwise religious piece. Nevertheless, in the earliest and most austere monument of Attic drama, the *Suppliants* of Aeschylus, not two but possibly as many as fifty girls are barely saved, by the timely arrival of the king, from being herded off into captivity and enforced marriage. Such scenes, in which a Greek prince prevents the incidence of barbarian outrage, or an Athenian ruler thwarts the highhandedness of an oligarchic authoritarian, embodied serious ideational contrasts for the Athenians of the fifth century. They were not mere action and excitement; they were commentaries on what it was felt Greek civilization was and should be, providing important evidence for the self-consciousness and world-outlook of the Athenians.

When Polyneices has departed, a roll of thunder, the sign for which Oedipus had waited, finally comes. It comes like the Sanctus Bell between the Ordinary and the Canon of the Mass, and it introduces a comparable communion between God and man. Oedipus sends hastily for Theseus, to whom he announces the hour of his death and gives final instructions. It is now the blind man's turn to lead. The dramatic effect of this moment is deeply thrilling. Oedipus, whose physical blindness and helplessness have been so carefully established throughout the play, now rises to his feet and without guidance from anyone present, leads the others into the sacred grove of the Eumenides. The rest is told by a messenger, how he prepared himself, tarrying until a mysterious voice called him by name, then bade farewell to his daughters, and unaccompanied save by Theseus, went into the most holy part of the glade and there was translated, while Theseus remained standing, shading his eyes from the unbearable vision of godhead. The play ends with a lyric scene, full of bereavement and yearning, as Antig-

one and Ismene mourn the loss of their father, and ask safe conduct back to Thebes. Then the chorus moves off singing a mysterious line:

> Weep not; for altogether, these things have authority.

If the *Oedipus at Colonus* fails to exhibit the dramatic alacrity of
earlier plays, it is for a good reason. The play presents the long slow
reversal of the *Oedipus Rex*. Instead of the abrupt plunge down the
precipice, the movement here is laboriously uphill, and endurance
is the criterion. The gods who speak from the whirlwind imparted
their lightning swiftness to the *Oedipus Rex*. Oedipus himself sets
the tempo for the play in which, hated by the gods and abandoned,
he finds his answer to them. The gods who destroyed him earlier
make no further move, either for or against him, until they finally
acknowledge his dignity with the affidavit of their heavenly thunder
and bring to pass the moment in which he is complete. The timeless divinities are the lords of time, but Oedipus is the actor, and
he looks to them for nothing save the continuation of their dread
function. If time continues, endurance continues; but while time
remains the same in essence, endurance grows greater, and so does
knowledge. Given time, tlemosyne must achieve its victory.

Almost in his first words, Oedipus lists time as one of the three
great elements of his moral fibre:

> Who will receive today the wanderer
> Oedipus, with some scanty charities?
> Who begs but little, and of that little still
> Gets less, but finds that it suffices him:
> For sufferings, and length of time, my comrade,
> And third, nobility, teach me content.

Previously, Oedipus had spoken of himself as the "brother of the
months." He now has time as his constant companion. Once time
had "found him out"; now it stands by him as a medium of greatness and even as a teacher. Again, as in the *Electra,* there is a contrast between what Oedipus is expected to learn from time and
what he actually does learn. In the scene with Creon, the latter,
staggered by Oedipus' proud replies, says that an old man in such
misery ought to have learned to be mild and acknowledge his own

weakness. But time teaches every man what he really is, and in Oedipus' case it has rather confirmed his high spirit and strength. It has, in a way, brought the man to pass, as it brings all things to pass, especially the most unexpected. Itself a paradox, time fosters paradox, and turns things into their opposites; it is the inevitable condition of Becoming, yet in the end it reveals Being, even as Oedipus implied to Theseus in the great speech already quoted. The gods are free of time, deathless and ageless. Yet in the world they govern, in the events wherein they manifest themselves, all things are inverted to their opposites, friend becomes enemy and enemy friend, faith dies, and falsehood blossoms. But the helpless and aged Oedipus, the prey of time, will become a timeless blessing, a member of those heroic dead whose power represented to the Greek mind one of the most holy and inviolable forces in the world.

This speech of Oedipus is somewhat reminiscent of Ajax's "yielding" speech, save that when Ajax says that in time things become their opposites, it is clear that he is resolved to be no more a part of the shoddy flux, but to get out of time, seize Being at a blow and be himself forever. The inflexible standard of the old arete compelled Ajax. But Oedipus' virtue was one of the intellect; like the Homeric Odysseus, he could accept time with its contradictions as the framework of man's existence in which through devious ways he comes to fulfillment. His inner law has made survival difficult, but necessary. For the same intellectual honesty and skill which drove him in the earlier play to find out who he was, and to boast that he could bear the knowledge, has given him both the will and the strength to achieve that boast.

Oedipus himself states clearly his moral independence of the gods in the scene with his daughter. Ismene has told him that the victory in the war depends on him, and Oedipus, half-aside, reflects on the strangeness of the news; Ismene tries to give a pious answer:

> *Ismene.* They say their victory lies in your hands.
> *Oedipus.* When I am nothing, then am I a man?
> *Ismene.* Yes, for the gods who smote now raise you up.
> *Oedipus.* Cheap gift, to raise an old man, who fell young!

The rejection of Ismene's pietism is unmistakable. A little later, when Ismene reports the prophecy that if Oedipus dies hostile to the Thebans his tomb will be an affliction to them, the old man, in deep self-consciousness of his inward power, says drily: "A man might know that by his wits, without a god's help." Indifferent to what the gods may seem to do, Oedipus trusts his intellect still; he does not really fancy the gods care about him at all. His exaltation cannot be interpreted as an act of grace, as Ismene suggests. It is a product from within, born of Oedipus' own equipment.

It has long since been recognized that Oedipus, in fundamental character, is still the same as ever. His mind, the quality which made him "small and great," has only been deepened, not discredited by time. No less his famous wrath is vigorous as of old, and perhaps even a little more savage, as the insight and authority which motivate it grow. Innocent sufferer though he may be, he shows none of the religious transfiguration or humble self-abnegation of the Christian martyr. Half of his exalted function is to bless Attica, but the other half is to have personal revenge on his enemies, and the terrible explosions which Creon and Polyneices endure show the ferocity of his hatred and anger; even Theseus gets a rather sharp answer. Christian sentiment may recoil from the sheer violence of these outbursts; but the hypocrisy which they rebuke need find no sympathy. Oedipus is more right than ever in his anger, for his honesty has only grown fiercer with the years. The compromise which all expected of a condemned and polluted exile has not been forthcoming.

For all that, it is never for a moment forgotten that Oedipus is polluted, that he is the man who slew his father and married his mother. Not only his character but also his external fate remains unchanged. To emphasize this point, Sophocles has symbolized it nicely in the first part of the play by making him once more stumble into defilement. The first thing he does is to step on the consecrated ground and sit on a sacred stone. Thus throughout the prologue, first chorus, and first episode, he is technically guilty of sacrilege against the Eumenides. Eventually he makes amends, or rather sends his daughter to make them; but he is in no hurry, and in the end, it is into the most sacred and forbidden part of the grove that he turns. By this light touch the poet recalls and reasserts the same old fate of Oedipus the king—his almost innate luck of touching things which are forbidden, without knowing it. He is the man who treads blindly and innocently upon taboos. Yet even as Oedipus had formerly committed sacrilege and survived in greater wisdom and strength, so now the revelation of his error does not cause him to start up in alarm; he only asks on what land he is trespassing:

> *Stranger.* Here the dread
> Goddesses dwell, daughters of Earth and Darkness.
> *Oedipus.* Let me hear by what name I should address them.
> *Stranger.* The people of this land call them the all-seeing
> Eumenides; elsewhere they've other names.
> *Oedipus.* Graciously let them take their suppliant
> For from this place I never shall depart.
> *Stranger.* What does this mean?
> *Oedipus.* The token of my fate.

The last line, like so many of Oedipus' remarks, is spoken as an aside and goes uncomprehended by the stranger, who at once changes the subject. But it is clear that Oedipus has passed beyond the phase where technical defilement matters. If it had been his fate alone of all men to defile what was most sacred and to suffer for it, his suffering has invested him with certain rights; for now he alone of all men may walk in the Athenian grove of the Furies and not suffer.

And what strange Furies these are, who receive their suppliant graciously—and such a suppliant—and whose grove echoes with the song of nightingales. These are purely Athenian Furies; only after the first consistory of the Areopagus were the Furies given nightingale voices, when an earlier exile, "hated of the gods," Orestes, found relief and dignity again in the equable air of Athens. Now Oedipus comes to Athens, and there is no yelping of "insatiable, bronze-footed bloodhounds," but only the music of the birds, as if all the past evil of the Theban house were transformed by the mysterious forces of time and suffering into a present of tranquil beauty and a prospect of hope. Quite after his own fashion, Sophocles has borrowed the gentle goddesses of pain from Aeschylus and spun them magically into his many-leveled, symbolic scheme of the heroic life. Here, in the grove of these paradoxically sweet dread goddesses, Oedipus could recognize a token of his fate; and Athens too could see herself once more, as at the trial of

Orestes, the defender of the weak, mediator between the suppliant
and justice, the restorer of the fallen—the great role she loved to
play. With characteristic finish, Sophocles brings in these nightingales again in the great ode on Athens, so that the whole episode
of Oedipus' coming and acceptance is rounded off with the music
of nightingales.

Error and exaltation, pollution and the song of nightingales!
No union of opposites could be more Sophoclean. Nothing is
denied or remitted; all the old misery, the horror of the fate of
Oedipus remains unchanged and unrationalized. Nothing has been
invented to show that the gods really meant well. Within and
without Oedipus is the same man, save that he has added a new
dimension of fortitude and knowledge. He continues to act his
role with ever increasing self-consciousness. He knows the "token
of his fate," and therein creates a historical self. He is the blind
man who knows; he is the "hated of God" who is innocent and
noble. In this role he will win recognition.

Oedipus' battle for significance finds its core in the defense of
his nobility. Those about him on the whole believe that no one
could do the things which he did and yet be a good man. The lack
of distinction which antiquity, until the time of Socrates, made between inner and outer values is well expressed in the famous
scolion of Simonides:

> No man can help being bad
> Whom hopeless misfortune seizes;
> For every man who fares well is good,
> But if he fares ill, he is bad; and the best on the whole
> Are those the gods love.

The gods had not loved Oedipus; he had been seized with hope-
less misfortune. Hence the chorus is suspicious of him from the
first. When they hear who he is, their reaction shows clearly how
they have formulated their feelings about him. He must be guilty,
for if his murder of Laius had been the moral equivalent of mere
manslaughter in self-defense, the gods would not have punished
him:

> No fated punishment comes to him
> Who avenges what he first has suffered.

The gods afflict him, he must be evil; let him get out. Antigone attempts to correct this attitude by presenting her father in the light of one undeservingly oppressed by the gods' arbitrary will:

> Among all men you will not find
> One who, if a god leads on,
> Has power to escape.

In these two views the fate of Oedipus is summarized respectively as a tragedy of fault and a tragedy of fate. Antigone's appeal is meant to lighten the burden of guilt, but only Oedipus himself understands fully his own innocence.

The *Oedipus Rex* can hardly have failed to stir ambiguous reactions in Athens. The passages just quoted illustrate the interpretations which his story prompts; indeed, it is even possible that between 429 and Sophocles' resumption of the myth, the much debated question of the guilt or innocence of Oedipus had already begun to divide readers into bristling camps. Sophocles may have wished to settle it once and for all by the heavy emphasis he lays in this play upon his hero's innocence. In his very opening speech, Oedipus mentions "suffering, time, and third, nobility" as the things which have given him his strength. The emphasis upon "nobility" is beyond question. Time and suffering will do nothing for the ignoble man, except make him bitter. Even as in the *Oedipus Rex,* when he faced the imminent revelation of his parricide and incest, he knew that no external fortune could destroy his soul, so now in his old age he maintains his basic excellence. Later, when Antigone's appeal has quieted the chorus, in a speech of formal defense, he states quite explicitly that his deeds were unwilled, and that his griefs are due to no evil in his nature:

> And will you then
> Uproot me from this seat and drive me forth,
> Fearing a name alone? You cannot fear
> Either my body or my deeds; for these
> My deeds were not committed; they were suffered,
> If, as you must, you mean my history,
> My father and my mother, for which tales
> You fear me. Ah, full well I know it is!
> And yet, how am I evil in my nature,

> I who, when struck, struck back, so that had I
> Even known my victim, I'd not be condemned.

The legal claim that he killed in self-defense and ignorance is backed by the moral claim that even if he had known that his assailant was his father, he would not be morally guilty. It will be remembered that Laius had hit him over the head with an ox-goad, for no reason other than that he was in the way, a fact which perhaps lends weight to Oedipus' claim. Be that as it may, the real innocence rests, in his own eyes, upon his inward conviction of integrity. Later he says to Creon:

> For not in me, not in myself, could you
> Discover any stain of sin, whereby
> I sinned against myself and mine.

Oedipus' rejection of the word "hamartia" here clearly has an inward reference, while his outer misdeeds are undeniable. In a similar spirit he can use the old figure of the "gift of the gods," always a dangerous thing to receive:

> *Chorus.*   You have done—
> *Oedipus.* I have not done.
> *Chorus.*   What then?
> *Oedipus.* I have received a gift. . .

The gods and their gifts, the misery of his life; these are all externals, and ineluctable. But he is himself, and the gods can do nothing to break the strong moral good he wills. Oedipus is a landmark in Greek morality, for he presents the first really clear exposition of the independence of the inner life, that doctrine which in Socrates and his followers became the cornerstone of a whole new phase of civilization.

Yet for this moral independence to be significant—to be real, one might say—it had to be recognized. Herein the feelings of the fifth-century poet differed from the mysticism of Plato, the reality of whose inner world was prior and causal. For Sophocles, the hero must win in this world; whether in such a death as Antigone's or in such a life as Oedipus', the heroic victory had all its reference and significance in the purely human sphere. Hence the rising action of the *Oedipus at Colonus* shows the hero's triumph over person after person. He already has Antigone, in whom for the first time a Sophoclean protagonist has a real companion. Antigone is not a foil, she is a counterpart to Oedipus; Sophocles kept in mind the character he had given her almost forty years before and here endowed her with no little of her father's endurance. Ismene shares her position to some extent, so that in the three of them, in the scenes where the old man praises his daughters, one detects the nucleus of a world in which Oedipus is acceptable and honored. With them, Oedipus stands on his own terms, commanding and receiving freely their love and honor.

It is not long before the stranger of the prologue adopts a respectful tone. The chorus similarly, in spite of its misgivings, is forced "to feel awe at his pronouncements." But the climax of Oedipus' triumph over society appears in the scene with Theseus, who recognizes him at once as a superior being. It is the essentially Athenian interpretation of arete which underlies this scene and makes it moving. Theseus represents Athens; without hesitation he penetrates all the disguises of fortune and circumstance and arrives at the true man. Drawn in the aristocratic colors of a legendary king, he is none the less the embodiment of the most enlightened kind of democratic individualism. Mutual recognition of virtue, as in the case of Philoctetes and Neoptolemus, can bring the great man back to the world, or, more accurately, can bring the world back to the great man, whose ethos has remained unchanged. The value of the true man, whatever his state, attains a just estimate in the liberal air of Athens. Theseus comes and listens respectfully before Oedipus, and Oedipus acknowledges his excellence. Hero recognizes hero as a fellow stranger in this world, knowing its uncertainty, and basing standards of behavior on its immanent sorrow. Oedipus makes for himself a world of the souls that can respect him in his tribulations, and when he departs, he is no longer isolated, but prized.

Thus, like Philoctetes, Oedipus is set free to bestow the value of himself upon the world. But those who would avail themselves of his blessing must accept the blind beggar himself and not try to use his greatness without understanding him. So too, Philoctetes' magic bow could not be separated from its lame and offensive owner. The paradox of human value must be taken whole; there is no short way. Philoctetes and disease are one; Oedipus and pollution are one. The hero's external daimon and internal daimon, that is, the inner and outer divine forces of his life, are inextricably interwoven until the great moment comes when the external yields, and the hero's inwardness may burst out and become a reality. And this is not so much a mystic process as a social one. Theseus and the Athenians could perceive that reality through the shell. They are therefore a little like Oedipus, who is blind but full of true insight: "All he says has eyes." His murmured remark, "When I am nothing, then am I a man?" conveys the whole secret. His triumph is prepared within himself, almost in defiance of the very gods themselves, and the Athenians, when they accept his paradox, are made worthy to share in his triumph.

But his triumph does not come without a struggle. The two scenes in which Oedipus sets his face against Thebes forever have occasioned much criticism. Their relevance has either been missed altogether, or else explained merely in connection with the original saga, the *fabula sacra*. But part of the saga is not necessarily part of the play. For the Greek dramatist, there was no *fabula sacra;* he was as free as Homer to exclude whatever detail he felt to be irrelevant. As examples of Oedipus' growing heroic powers, wherewith he settles his accounts in the world, the episodes of Creon and Polyneices clearly contribute something to the character of the protagonist; but their significance is greater than that. The moral essence of these scenes is derived from the problem of the *Philoctetes,* where an individual of heroic proportions, rejected long since and cast away by his comrades, becomes once more the object of their specific personal concern.

Over and over again we are told that the Thebans, and Creon in particular, had exiled Oedipus long after the latter had ceased to feel that exile was necessary or appropriate to his misfortunes; up till that time they had kept him against his will. Precisely why is a question. Euripides, in the closing scene of the *Phoenissae,* makes the exile of Oedipus begin after the expedition of the Seven is over; it is therefore an act of the new king, Creon, who perhaps may be thought to have planned it in order to consolidate his power. In Sophocles' play, however, Oedipus was exiled while Creon was merely regent, during the minority of the princes. The latter, apparently, had been quite passive in the matter. In the absence of conclusive evidence, it is perhaps safe to assume that the disposal of Oedipus in some way affected the various claimants' interest in the throne. In any case, the very doubtfulness of the motivation suggests Sophocles' real intention: the Thebans had used the legally justifiable reason for exile, blood guilt, as a kind of political cover for more selfish motives. Oedipus himself seems to feel that he ought to be received into Thebes and buried there. Yet technically, as a parricide, Oedipus could not possibly return. The Thebans certainly had no intention of bringing him into the city, but only of keeping him near at hand. One might well ask how it had been possible for him to stay in the first place, and why he thought he might return at all, if ritual pollution had really such a solemn significance.

But the fact is, such pollution was open to flexible treatment, and the sons of Oedipus and Creon had made political capital of it. And now, like Odysseus in the *Philoctetes,* Creon and Polyneices both wish to use the great man's power without accepting the man himself. The oracle told them they would conquer if they could get him back, but there is yet some question of how a hero must be received. The great contrast with the pragmatic scheme of the Thebans is the frank and generous attitude of Theseus. Not only does he feel a personal respect and kinship for Oedipus; he gives him the full rights of a citizen and even offers to take him to his own house. With Theseus' example before them, even the choristers seem no longer to fear the pollution which attends the old man, and they defend him valiantly against Creon's attack. To be sure, the Athenians are to gain much from him, but they have not tried to achieve it by the half-and-half plan of Creon.

In the scene with Creon, the political substance of the play becomes most clear, and brings the elements of festival drama into the foreground. All that the Athenian mind felt to be politically good clashes openly with the spiritual blindness of Creon. Creon arrives in guile and departs in violence. He behaves like a tyrant— indeed, he calls himself one—and he carries off women, as tyrants are supposed to do. But he is also much subtler, and like most fifth-century stage tyrants, he possesses less in common with the economic dictators of history than with the clever, sophistically

trained oligarchs of the war years. His obsequious carefulness before
the Athenian choristers who, by a curious anachronism, are at once
the subjects of Theseus and liberal exponents of democracy, includes not only respectful compliments, but even a passing inti-
mation that he represents a majority vote. With deft political skill
he answers the arraignment of Theseus by trying to use Athenian
institutions and the famous piety of Athens to his own advantage:
he says smoothly that he is sure that Athens would never receive an
unholy incestuous parricide; the Areopagus would never allow it.
Creon seems to know well the principle formulated later by Aristotle, that "we should know the moral qualities characteristic of
each form of government, for the special moral character of each
is found to provide us with our most effective means of persuasion
in dealing with it."

Aristotle further states that the end of tyranny is protection of
the tyrant, while the end of aristocracy is the maintenance of education and national institutions. Clearly Creon is here a tyrant
speaking in his own defense; but with great skill he uses as his principal argument the moral end of the aristocratic Theseus, namely
the maintenance of Athenian piety and the court of the Areopagus.
A definite political antinomy, therefore, is only thinly veiled in this
scene. It appears even more clearly in Theseus' reproof, which
enters almost unnecessarily into Theban manners. Creon, says
Theseus, is not only unworthy of Athens, but unworthy of Thebes
herself, and the Theban tradition of breeding gentlemen.

By contrast with Creon, the failed aristocrat, the mythic figure
of Theseus, characterized both as the true aristocrat and the man
of the polis, with its ideal of legality and true piety, points the
religious question implicit in the political antinomy. Creon's well-
planned references to Athenian piety miss fire. Theseus deigns no
answer, but Oedipus in towering wrath bursts out in one of his
terrible cannonades. He defends himself from the scornful, personal taunts of Creon, strips the veil from his pretense of justice,
and then says:

> How fine for you to flatter Theseus' name
> And Athens, calling her well administered!
> But in your commendations you miss much;

> If any land knows how to honor gods,
> With reverence, this land leads all the rest.
> Wherefrom you, plundering these girls and me,
> The aged suppliant, try to drag us off!

Creon's breach of the most holy right of the aged and the suppliant fits oddly with his otherwise scrupulous observance of religious forms in treating a parricide. He will bring Oedipus into the vicinity of Thebes as a useful object, but will not admit his technical pollution within the walls. The Thebans are thus represented as standing on the forms of piety without regarding their essence, while Athens "knows how to honor the gods with reverence," by receiving the suppliant generously with no reservations. Far from dallying over mere religious formalities, Theseus leaves a sacrifice half-finished in order to go to battle for his guests—the sort of religious enlightenment which Sparta, for instance, would not risk in the crucial year of Marathon.

These details are too closely allied to the play's principal action to be regarded as merely adventitious. The paradox of seeming and being, which informs the character of the hero, is here extended to include a commentary on the spirit and the letter, in the culture and political ethics of Greece herself. In this scene, even more fully than in the great ode on Athens, Sophocles has poured out his love for the city and his faith in her as the genuine polis, where not merely the nightingales sing and the sacred olives flourish, but where also the individual man, that irreducible minimum of political or any other kind of greatness, holds his place by arete alone, and "whatever good he may do the city."

Scholars have long since recognized references to the Peloponnesian War in this play. The shadow of bitter hatred between Athens and Thebes overhangs the whole, and with reason, for in the late years of the war, Thebes showed herself Athens' most implacable enemy, ransacking her outlying fields for anything movable, and clamoring later at the peace table for demolition of her walls and enslavement of her inhabitants. In the years just preceding Arginusae (406), when the *Oedipus at Colonus* was written, Athens was in desperate condition. The treasury was empty, the statues stripped of their gold; her leaders were incompetent, her population starving, every nerve was strained to the breaking point.

If Thucydides, writing probably at about this same time, could call
Athens "the education of Greece," because she represented the
greatest opportunity for an individual to be self-sufficient and at
his best, it is not so surprising that Sophocles too, with his pro-
fundity of poetic insight, should have been able to see his city
historically and create a vision of her which would be as timeless
as the heroism of the old Oedipus. When he speaks of Athens in
the play, he never mentions her sufferings. He speaks of her as if
she were inviolable, as if the sacred olive trees were not burned
stumps and the land ravaged and ruined. Athens herself in those
days was a pattern of heroic tlemosyne; and if Sophocles could see
beyond the ruins and the stumps, it was because he saw whence
Athens derived her almost incredible fortitude. The value of man
was implicit in it all, and embodied in the figure of Oedipus. The
man whose intellect has brought him to divine insight has come to
the place where only the true counts. The ideal Athenian setting
is more than a patriotic motif: in it Sophocles symbolizes the world
of man's metaphysical value, the world which is the only home for
Oedipus. The picture is, of course, confessedly and purposely ideal-
ized, but it is not fiction. It is myth, which is to say, it is history
distilled into meaning.

The scene with Polyneices completes the picture of society's mis-
guided attempt to regain the great individual for its own ends.
Once more, as in the *Philoctetes,* the attempt through guile and
force yields to the attempt through persuasion and appeal, and
once more the same refusal follows. Polyneices is no mere politician
like Creon; he is very sympathetically drawn. Even though he is
perhaps still too self-involved to rise above his practical need of
Oedipus into a full understanding of the old man's worth, nevertheless his full admission of guilt, and especially his recognition
that has come too late, stamp him at once as a serious and wellnigh
tragic character. Therefore the appalling execrations which the
old man calls down on him are the more surprising. But Polyneices
really is too late, and it is only out of empty hope that he can
suggest how he may make up for his sins.

For Polyneices' faults are in his nature and in the nature of his
will. He has put himself where he cannot turn back, but he has
done so not because of any moral standard, but because he wanted

the throne. He is therefore in a tragic situation, perhaps, but he is not a tragic character; however genuine his penitence may be, it implies little understanding and no real morality. Fundamentally he needs Oedipus for precisely the same reason as Creon does, and he would never have come otherwise. Oedipus' refusal of him rests on the same absolute standard he had always espoused. Since now Oedipus is himself all but a god, it may be said that his refusal rests on a divine standard.

The curse may seem another matter. Many scholars have argued that Oedipus was wrong to curse his son; others that the curse merely illustrates Oedipus' great exaltation. Still others have collected much juridical evidence to prove that Polyneices, as the very image of a bad son, by all contemporary standards deserved damnation. Yet in a play about inner and outer religious standards, Sophocles would hardly allow Polyneices to be condemned on merely legalistic grounds. Polyneices is undoubtedly a bad son; yet he is drawn in touchingly human colors: in his parting from Antigone, in his rather high conception of generalship, and in the loneliness of his sorrow as he bravely accepts his fate, he carries away a good deal of our sympathy. The simply bad son might be forgiven, one feels, if Antigone could intercede for him. If Sophocles meant us to remember only his past deeds, he should have made him appear more like them. But instead, he has deliberately given his cause some justice by making him the elder, instead of the younger brother.

It has been wisely noted that in the epic source the curse on the sons of Oedipus precedes and apparently causes their strife, but in Sophocles the strife came first, arising "from some god and their own sinful mind." By the time Oedipus utters his curse, Polyneices is already on his way to the war, and is too fatally involved to turn back, as his words to Antigone show. So the curse, which once had a supernatural causative force, is here simply a statement of fact, though Polyneices still refers to the Furies as the ones who will bring it to pass, as one always speaks of a god in connection with what is true. Obviously it is Polyneices who will bring it to pass, for he is already doing it, and Sophocles has made it doubly pointed by letting Antigone beg him so movingly to desist. But Polyneices, whose name means the "man of the heavy curse," knows who he is.

Quite aside from his past cruelty to his father and sister, and even apart from the fact that he is still only trying to use Oedipus, Polyneices deserves the curse because he is accursed, as Esau was accursed long before the actual denunciation came. Oedipus, like an oracle, has simply told the truth. Once more, the supernatural element enters in such a way that it can only be symbolic. Appropriately enough, the last of the three gods whom Oedipus invokes to destroy Polyneices is the War itself, the really destructive element "which has cast such heavy strife" between the brothers.

The Creon and Polyneices scenes are not loosely or poorly integrated, from the moral point of view. From the mere standpoint of plot they revive and restate the conflicts of the *Philoctetes,* illustrating with infinitely subtle turns the world with which the great individual must deal, in his struggle for weight, dignity, and reality. Individualism in terms of such values means more than ordinary individualism; it is a norm of heroic being. And the basic difference between Oedipus and Polyneices is that Oedipus asserts his heroic right to be, while Polyneices asserts only his right to have. Therefore the one is oracular and blessed, the other accursed and pathetically confused in his humanity.

With the retreat of Polyneices, Oedipus' moral triumph is complete, and the mastery which he has shown throughout the play is now symbolized in the final scene of divine mastery. The last and most impressive of the supernatural happenings in Sophocles has this in common with all the others: the supernatural "cause" follows its effect. Oedipus officially "becomes a hero," with the power of blessing and cursing. But manifestly, the transformation which takes place in the depth of the sacred grove adds little in itself to the power of Oedipus. The blind and aged hero has already repulsed Creon and cursed Polyneices; before he leaves, he pronounces the eternal blessing upon Theseus and Attica. To the Greek, a person could become a hero only if he really was one, and Oedipus has already exercised his full prerogatives. Viewed in their simplest and most profound light, these prerogatives are no more than the ability to see through the veils of circumstance into essential fact. Oedipus' words all "have eyes." His insight attains its perfect symbol when he himself leads the way into the grove, unguided except by what he calls "the present deity"; nor does he hesitate to

identify himself subtly with that divine force. The inward man has
at last come true.

It is a grave mistake to overlook the moral qualities which have
made Oedipus a hero, and to regard his apotheosis as a simple act
of grace on the part of the gods, or as amends made by them for
the sufferings which he has endured. The choristers, indeed, interpret it thus:

> Out of the many woes that came
> Without cause, now the god in justice
> Would lift him up.

On the other hand, they have already prayed on their own behalf,
when they heard the thunder and saw Oedipus' fate coming, to be
delivered from any share in such "gainless grace." It is clear that
they regard the gods as the actors here, and the whole process as
fraught with danger, not only for Oedipus, but also for the passive
spectators. These good Athenians, with their simple, human limitations and their sophrosyne, know that the gods can be almost as
perilous friends as they are enemies, and they would prefer to stand
apart and pray. Oedipus himself rejects any such interpretation,
however. He uses the word "grace," but always of the blessing he
himself is to bestow on Athens.

It will be remembered with what contempt he treated the suggestion of Ismene, in an earlier scene, when she remarked that the
gods who formerly destroyed him were now about to reinstate him.
Oedipus, with his customary brutal truthfulness, called it a cheap
favor. Indeed, the gods did little for Oedipus; he had to prove himself every inch of the way, and it is no wonder that he omits all
sanctimonious expressions of gratitude. He speaks seriously of the
gods and the world at large only to Theseus, for the latter is the
only other character of sufficiently heroic proportions to understand
him in his own terms. By the same token, Theseus alone is permitted to witness the last hour of Oedipus. Only the large soul
can fully understand how "the gods look well but late," how time
penetrates all things, or how the noblest in man is rooted in his
essential weakness and subjection to change. Others may grasp the
words when they are spoken, but Theseus comprehends out of his
own being. And Theseus, champion of the true Athenian religi-

osity, regards Oedipus himself as the grace-bringer, not the gods. There was no Messiah in Greek theology; if man was to come near to the divine, he must get there himself. How this can be achieved is known only to him who has in some sense already achieved it; the rest of the world will view it with limited, and doubtless frightened, eyes. As Hölderlin once wrote:

> Only those who themselves are
> Godlike ever believe in gods.

Oedipus brings us to a vision of godhead, whose content and significance are Oedipus himself. Sophocles says nothing of the gods who greet him, but he has shown all he could of the man who, after long sorrow, greeted the gods.

The end, therefore, is no great change, except that it releases Oedipus from the struggle of asserting himself and the suffering which pursued the moral activity of his soul. He had exalted himself by his endurance in that activity, and the final scene shows only the universal of which the play was the particular. That universal is all important, but one must not forget how it came about. It is the result of "time, suffering, and his own nobility." How perfectly his last words to his daughters sum up the trial of values by which he has triumphed:

> Children, it now behoves you leave this place,
> Enduring, in nobility of mind.

Endurance, nobility, mind: these are the laws of the human soul. So stated, they sound very simple, and in essence perhaps they are. But in action—which is life, and the only context in which human beings can know them—they are the stuff of tragedy, the divine scheme or *ananke* which binds the magnanimous man to himself and puzzles and outrages the philistine world, until it finally can ratify itself in a form that can no longer be denied.

To the audience which first witnessed the *Oedipus at Colonus* the conviction must have inevitably come that this was not the end of the hero, but his real beginning. The eye involuntarily follows him out of sight, and creates its own image of what happened thereafter. The simple fact that Oedipus became one of the lesser, though doubtless more revered, local deities can never account for Sophocles' having written this long, complex work, with its keenly dramatized distinctions between inner and outer, and its iridescent interplay of godlike and manlike qualities in the central figure. Sophocles must seek what the process of becoming a hero included for Oedipus himself; how and why the fallen—for Oedipus is in this play, as much as before, Everyman—can still achieve an inch of significance and grow before our eyes, though the weight of the unyielding, and to ancient eyes, divine forces seemed forever pressing downward.

The *Oedipus at Colonus* ends with an apocalypse which, together with some other lines in Sophocles, illustrates to some extent the fifth century's outlook on both hero cults and death in general. There is, for instance, a passage in the *Electra,* where the chorus, attempting to console the heroine for her brother's supposed death, says:

> I know that the king Amphiaraus,
> Betrayed by the golden wiles of woman, lies buried;
> And now under the earth
> All-shade he rules.

In this difficult passage, the reference to Amphiaraus is clear enough, but there is considerable question of its relevance. The famous warrior-prophet, who was betrayed into joining the Seven against Thebes by his wife Eriphyle, seems to have little to do with Orestes. And what does the last line mean—"All-shade he rules"? The word translated "all-shade" (πάμψυχος) occurs only here, and the scholiast, confused but generous, offers three explanations: "Either," he says, taking it as "all-soul" rather than "all-shade," "he rules over all the souls, which stand in need of his prophetic art"—referring presumably to the souls of the living who consulted his oracle near Thebes; for the shades of the dead have little need of prophecy—"or, he is 'all-soul' because he saved his whole soul; or, because throughout everything he keeps his soul, which is immortal." The idea that famous heroes become rulers among the dead is as old as Homer; hence the scholiast's first suggestion is the one generally accepted. Although this does not seem quite right, still the general meaning of the lines is clear. It is a contrast

between the fact of death and the fact of ruling. Death has not
deprived Amphiaraus of his eminence, but has given him an eternal
though shadowy royalty. Therefore, it is implied that, in a similar
way, though Orestes is dead, his arete still holds its place in the
world of the shades.

Does this imply the immortality of the soul? The scholiast barely
suggested the idea, and few would care to defend it. Yet the juxta-
position of death and power implies something; the paradox is
pregnant with faith in the indestructible value of human nobility.
Added to the other passages in which the inner divinity of the protagonist shows itself, these lines form one more link in the chain
of Sophoclean humanism which sees godhead operative in the moral
being of man. The Niobe passages of Antigone and Electra, the
latter's reference to the present deity in Orestes, Philoctetes' vision
of his patron god, the passage on Amphiaraus, and old Oedipus' departure from the stage unguided save by "the present god"—all
these, and perhaps more, point steadily in one direction: toward
a verity in human life which is, or at least becomes, immutable—
a particular which becomes general and attains to the authority
of a historical truth.

And for this truth, in what was perhaps the last line of poetry
he ever wrote, Sophocles used the word *kyros* (κῦρος), which indicates a universally ratified authority: "Weep not, for altogether
these things have authority [*kyros*]." That which is conceived to be
at once authoritative and universal was to the Greeks divine: the
gods were divine, law was divine; certain aspects of nature, even
aside from conscious or developed animism, had their own divinity
—the sea, the earth, the sun. Not superstition but religious intuition lies in such terminology, for it is almost a way of saying that
these things really exist and are wonderful—even as the Ionian philosophers equated real being with "the divine" or "godhead."
Therefore when Sophocles says that the fate of Oedipus has complete *kyros*, he means that he has passed into the realm of what
is universal, true, and authoritative, and so divine. His inner divinity is forever ratified and preserved. For Electra and Antigone,
the universal symbol was Niobe; for Philoctetes, Heracles; for
Orestes, perhaps Amphiaraus, in a lesser way. The ancient classic
example, or *paradeigma,* was thus extended into a religious token

or symbol. In the *Ajax,* this technique was not yet developed, and in the *Trachiniae* the faith that impelled it was lost. But Oedipus, who even in the earlier play could call himself the brother of the months, in the end dwarfs all the earlier heroes by becoming his own symbol. It had taken Sophocles ninety years of spiritual struggle, probing the depths of human evil, to see man finally in such a light.

Without the aid of doctrine, dogma, or formal creed, and without the weighty deliberation of ecumenical councils, a poet is not apt to evolve a system. Sophocles did not. His work is the truer therefore; all the paradoxes remain; nothing is oversimplified, and equally, nothing is explained by the cathedral-like rationale of a static theology. Experience for the poet remains fluid and valid; it crystallizes, if at all, only into myth and poetry, both of which are imperishable but plastic. Wherever the experience of the individual soul becomes important, there the value of society's systems is called in question and eventually relegated to a position of merely formal, social importance, if not altogether overthrown. The Italian Renaissance, of course, is the perfect illustration, and the works of Sophocles, seen in the light of their spiritual and humanistic import, gain still a new degree of incandescence when set beside the emotional stirrings of the Renaissance. There again faith in the individual becomes heroic, experience becomes at once illuminated and mysterious, the state religion recedes coldly before the intuition of human beauty and excellence and only glows for the last time when a fair lady guides an intensely personal and sensuous poet through its labyrinthine levels.

It is never easy to say what exactly is the content of humanistic faith. It is as broad as human experience; its core is moral, and it becomes authoritative and universal. But it is hard to say more. In Sophocles' plays, various specific elements have presented themselves; but as a whole, the underlying humanistic faith is an emotional and poetic one, most akin to the intuitive passion of the Renaissance. And indeed it is not surprising, on the brink of a great Enlightenment, where the blankest superstition may stand side by side with utter skepticism, that the men who most fully embody the spirit of their age should give themselves to neither, but on their own behalf seek out and evolve, not cautious middle ground, but a truly perspicuous faith. It is more wonderful that so plastic a religious attitude, at once passionate and refined, should be able for a brief period to flood the interstices of early disintegration in a culture where the canons of a powerful and once-satisfying orthodoxy and the aspirations of the individual's destiny have begun to diverge. Perhaps the finest commentary available on the work of Sophocles, and on the victory of Oedipus in particular, is to be found in the famous work on the *Dignity of Man* by Pico, Count of Mirandola. It would be dangerous to assume a direct connection; but in 1423, Giovanni Aurispa sent the great Laurentian manuscript of Sophocles to Niccolo de' Niccoli, a famous Florentine bibliophile, and three quarters of a century later, Pico wrote:

> I created thee (God is speaking to man) a being neither heavenly nor earthly, neither mortal nor immortal only, that thou mightest be free to shape and to overcome thyself. Thou mightest sink into a beast, and be born anew to the divine likeness. The brutes bring from their mother's body what they will carry with them as long as they live; the higher spirits are from the beginning, or soon after, what they will be for ever. To thee alone is given a growth and a development depending on thine own free will. Thou bearest in thee the germs of a universal life.

It is the germ of this universal life which in *Oedipus at Colonus* has come to full flower. The status of the chthonian hero, the dead *numen* in the earth, aptly symbolizes, as doubtless it did from the beginning, man's special partaking of death and life, of the transient and eternal.

Chronology of Important Dates

496 B.C.	Sophocles born at Colonus, village just outside Athens.
490	Greek victory over Persians at Marathon.
480	Greek victory over Persians at Salamis.
468	Sophocles' first victory in tragic competition, defeating Aeschylus.
458	Aeschylus' *Oresteia* (probably his last extant work).
447?	*Ajax.*
443-42	Sophocles elected steward of the Imperial Treasury.
442 or 441	*Antigone.*
440	Sophocles elected one of ten generals, with Pericles.
438	Euripides' *Alcestis* (probably his earliest extant work).
430s?	*Women of Trachis.*
431	Beginning of Peloponnesian war; Pericles in power.
430	Outbreak of plague in Athens.
425?	*Oedipus Rex.*
425	Aristophanes' *Acharnians* (his earliest extant work).
420	Sophocles receives cult of Asclepius on its arrival in Athens.
410s?	*Electra.*
413	Sophocles elected a special commissioner after Athenian defeat in Sicily.
409	*Philoctetes.*
406	Sophocles dies; cult founded to worship him as hero.
401	*Oedipus at Colonus* produced by Sophocles' grandson.

Notes on the Editor and Authors

THOMAS WOODARD, editor of this volume, received his Ph.D. in Comparative Literature from Harvard University, taught there and at Princeton University, and now lives in France.

SETH BENARDETE received his Ph.D. from the University of Chicago. While holding a Junior Fellowship at Harvard University he delivered a series of Lowell Lectures on Herodotus. He has taught at St. John's College and at Brandeis University.

SIGMUND FREUD analyzed a number of literary works, such as *The Brothers Karamazov* and *Hamlet,* along with such everyday symbolic occurrences as dreams and jokes.

MARTIN HEIDEGGER, the most influential German philosopher of the century, moved from the existential phenomenology of *Being and Time* (1928) to the poetic phenomenology of essays on Hölderlin, Plato, the Pre-Socratics, and others.

BERNARD M. W. KNOX taught the Classics at Yale University until he became Director of the Center for Hellenic Studies in Washington, D.C.

ROBERT D. MURRAY, JR., Professor of Classics at Princeton University, is especially interested in Greek lyric poetry and tragedy. He wrote *The Motif of Io in the Suppliants of Aeschylus.*

FRIEDRICH NIETZSCHE was a professor of classical philology at Basel for ten years before devoting himself exclusively to his philosophical works.

CHARLES PAUL SEGAL received his Ph.D. in Classics at Harvard University. After holding a Prix de Rome he taught at Harvard and is now Associate Professor of Classics at the University of Pennsylvania. He has published essays on the *Odyssey,* Pindar, Euripides, Vergil, and other subjects.

OSWALD SPENGLER's great work on the life cycle of civilizations draws on a wealth of imaginative analogues and antitheses and includes observations on most of the major works of art and literature.

CEDRIC WHITMAN, Professor of Greek Literature at Harvard University, has written important books on Homer and Aristophanes as well as Sophocles.

VIRGINIA WOOLF, the English novelist, showed her scope of literary appreciation in *Orlando,* the two *Common Readers,* and other critical essays.

Selected Bibliography

Translations

Fitts, Dudley, and Robert Fitzgerald, *The Oedipus Cycle*. New York: Harcourt, Brace and World, Inc., 1959. A Harvest paperback.

Grene, David, and Richmond Lattimore, Editors, *The Complete Greek Tragedies*, Vol. II. Chicago: University of Chicago Press, 1959. Also a Phoenix paperback and in The Modern Library.

Pound, Ezra, *Women of Trachis: a version*. London: Spearman, 1956.

Yeats, William Butler, *King Oedipus* and *Oedipus at Colonus*. *The Collected Plays*. London: Macmillan & Co., Ltd., 1953.

Interpretations

Fergusson, Francis, *The Idea of a Theater*, Chap. 1. Garden City: Doubleday & Co., Inc., 1949.

Goheen, Robert F., *The Imagery of Sophocles' Antigone: a Study of Poetic Language and Structure*. Princeton: Princeton University Press, 1951.

Kitto, H. D. F., *Greek Tragedy*, Chaps. V-VII, X, XIII. New York: Barnes and Noble, Inc., 3rd edition, 1961. The 2nd edition is in paperback, Doubleday Anchor Books, 1954.

———, *Form and Meaning in Drama*, Chaps. 4-6. New York: Barnes and Noble, Inc., 1957. Also a University paperback.

———, *Sophocles: Dramatist and Philosopher: Three Lectures*. London: Oxford University Press, 1958.

Knox, Bernard M. W., "Sophocles' Oedipus." In *Tragic Themes in Western Literature*. New Haven: Yale University Press, 1955.

———, *Oedipus at Thebes*. New Haven: Yale University Press, 1957.

———, *The Heroic Temper: Studies in Sophoclean Tragedy*. Berkeley: University of California Press, 1964.

Reinhardt, Karl, *Sophokles*. Frankfurt: Klostermann, 1947.

178

Weil, Simone, *Intuitions Pré-Chrétiennes,* pp. 15-20. Paris: La Colombe, 1951.

——, *La Source Grecque,* pp. 47-62. Paris: Gallimard, 1953.

Whitman, Cedric H., *Sophocles: a Study of Heroic Humanism.* Cambridge, Mass.: Harvard University Press, 1951.

Wilson, Edmund. "Philoctetes: the Wound and the Bow." In *The Wound and the Bow.* New York: Oxford University Press, Inc., 1965. A Galaxy paperback.

TWENTIETH CENTURY VIEWS

European Authors

TWENTIETH CENTURY VIEWS

American Authors

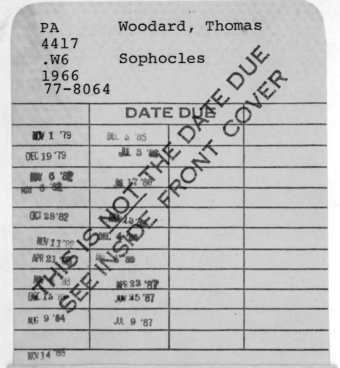